FANTASM AND FICTION

D0814686

Cultural Memory

in

the

Present

Mieke Bal and Hent de Vries, Editors

FANTASM AND FICTION

On Textual Envisioning

Peter Schwenger

STANFORD UNIVERSITY PRESS

STANFORD, CALIFORNIA

1999

Stanford University Press
Stanford, California
© 1999 by the Board of Trustees of the
Leland Stanford Junior University

Printed in the United States of America

CIP data appear at the end of the book

To the moveable feast:
Chris
Rhoda
Rachel
Maureen
Ann
Maurice
Alvin
&
Steven

Acknowledgments

Portions of this book have been published, in different form, in *Textual Practice*, *Studies in Romanticism*, *The University of Toronto Quarterly*, and *English Studies in Canada*.

I would like to thank Helen Tartar, Pamela MacFarland Holway, and Andrew Frisardi at Stanford University Press for their exemplary handling of the manuscript.

The process of research and writing has been supported throughout by a grant from the Social Sciences and Humanities Research Council of Canada. This funding made possible a series of research assistants, all remarkable: Kathleen McConnell, Emily Givner, and Mark Silverberg were beautifully attuned to the aims of my project, and much expanded my range.

An Internal Research Grant from Mount St. Vincent University allowed me to spend a week at the Ruth and Marvin Sackner Archive of Concrete and Visual Poetry in Miami Beach, in pursuit of what became Chapter 4 of this book. The riches of the Sackners' collection, combined with their generosity and knowledge, made this week not just useful but positively incandescent.

I owe to Ellen Esrock and Christopher Collins the stimulation of their own work on literary visualization, as well as their encouragement and criticism of mine.

David L. Clark, Christopher Heppner, and David Perkins read the essay on Romantic envisioning that became Chapter 5, and that their own work had helped to call into being.

Jack Zipes and Anna Kuhn encouraged and enriched my reading of Christa Wolf.

Eric Savoy introduced me to Wojnarowicz; Ann Krane guided me through psychology; Maureen McNeil read and critiqued "Dream Book."

And Steven Bruhm has read so many sections of this book, in so many versions, that I've lost count. For his support, and his thoughtful resistances, the only return I can make is to promise that I'll do the same for him.

P.S.

Contents

Illustrations

Thus, in a book picked up
From the ruins, you see a world erupt
And glitter with its distant sleepy past,
Green times of creatures tumbled to the vast
Abyss and backward: the brows of women,
An earring fixed with a trembling hand, pearl button
On a glove, candelabra in the mirror.

CZESLAW MILOSZ, "A BOOK IN THE RUINS"

We tried to see something, little by little we could almost see,
almost nothing was visible,
already something other than nothing
was visible in the almost.

JORIE GRAHAM, "HOLY SHROUD"

Entering the Book

I got a B on the first essay I wrote for my freshman English course—
"B" for Bemused, perhaps. The topic had been Jane Austen's *Emma*, and I
concluded my essay with an analysis of the scene in which the loathsome
Mr. Elton proposes to Emma during a carriage ride through a wintry
night. I dwelt on the ways that the mental agitation of the scene is mirrored by its physical qualities: the dash of snow against the carriage windows; the jolting of the carriage on the uneven road; the fitful illumination
of the carriage lamps, catching at intervals the violet silk lining of Emma's
bonnet. Not one of these details is to be found in Austen's text. I had in a
sense entered the book, imaginatively participated in it, and recorded what
I had seen. The essay got the grade it did because I needed to learn that visualization is not interpretation—at least, not as interpretation was then
interpreted. Yet a couple of years before I wrote my 1960 freshman essay,
Vladimir Nabokov was telling his students at Cornell what is demanded of
readers: "We must see things and hear things, we must visualize the rooms,
the clothes, the manners of an author's people. The color of Fanny Price's
eyes in *Mansfield Park* and the furnishing of her cold little room are important."[1] Once again, neither of these details is found in the text; Austen
has nothing to say about Fanny's eyes or the furnishing of her room.

For Nabokov, this kind of filling-in of fictional worlds was a necessary part of the full reading experience. For most literary critics it was
anathema, posing a real threat to any discipline with claims to rigor. The

discipline's very objects of study lose their coherence and autonomy, evaporating into impressionistic mist. And about impressions, merely *as* impressions, there can be no scholarly debate. When later in the 1960's the autonomy of the text was questioned, it was through rigorous procedures like deconstruction. This turn to hermeneutics left as far behind as ever the fantasmatic images generated by fiction. Only reader-response theory indicated a creative role for a reader who is always partly an author—though what was created was an experiential "meaning" rather than any experience of the senses.

In the early 1990's, however, there has been a turn back to the fantasmatic filling-in that fiction generates. That turn is exemplified by such works as Christopher Collins's *The Poetics of the Mind's Eye* and *Reading the Written Image*, both published in 1991; Ellen Esrock's 1994 study *The Reader's Eye*; and Elaine Scarry's 1995 essay "On Vivacity." Each of these scholars approaches the complex problem of visualization in a different way. What they have in common, though, is a certain philosophical slant: rather than discussing the specific visual content created by readers filling in a text—which of course is endlessly varied—they theorize the process of visual filling-in.

This turn toward the question of literary visualization is taking place within a larger "pictorial turn" in literary studies.[2] To some degree this is a re-turn to concerns that can be found intermittently in literary history, but which for us have become merely the road not taken—though it may be taken now. Mieke Bal begins a recent essay thus: "Some ten years ago, like many of us I believed in theory in a different way from today."[3] She goes on to describe her shift from semiotics to what she calls a "visual poetics," concerned with the reading of pictures. The pictures of reading, the "poetics of the mind's eye," can lead to a similar shift in theoretical emphasis. In Collins's terms, we are moving from hermeneutics to poetics, emphasizing the ways that a reader *performs* a text: for one of the greatest pleasures of reading is the pleasure of construction. Notwithstanding my emphasis on such construction, certain deconstructionist texts by Jacques Derrida have been enormously helpful in reminding me of the paradoxical strangeness that characterizes any reader's constructive act. And deconstructive thinkers often make some surprising turns of their own. Maurice Blanchot, who has eloquently explicated the "writing of disaster," sees reading (in his essay by that name) very differently: it is a "light, innocent

Yes," oblivious to the author's tortured processes. The mission of reading is to transform the book: "to make it transparent, to dissolve it with the penetration of a gaze which enthusiastically goes beyond it."[4] This dissolving gaze of the reader does not yield only an abysmal emptiness; rather, the page's underlying emptiness is shaped and supplemented, enthusiastically, until it generates simulacra of sensation.

Indeed the page may already have been shaped by such an enthusiastic envisioning, the marks on the page serving both as record and evocation of something that remains unmarked. Authors of fiction must envision their scenes before they find the words to convey them, and some of those authors are remarkably eloquent about the near-hallucinatory nature of that process, as we shall see. Even authors who are rather more reserved may hint at their visionary practice. It seems likely that Jane Austen, for instance, imagined far more physical detail than she allowed herself to include in the text. A letter to her sister Cassandra mentions attending an exhibition of paintings which, though not an especially good one, allowed Austen to indulge in what seems to have been a favorite game of hers, looking for likenesses of her own characters:

I was very well pleased—particularly (pray tell Fanny) with a small portrait of Mrs. Bingley, excessively like her. I went in hopes of seeing one of her Sister, but there was no Mrs. Darcy;—perhaps however, I may find her in the Great Exhibition which we shall go to, if we have time; . . . Mrs. Bingley's is exactly herself, size, shaped face, features & sweetness; there never was a greater likeness. She is dressed in a white gown, with green ornaments, which convinces me of what I had always supposed, that green was a favourite colour with her. I dare say Mrs. D. will be in Yellow.[5]

In *Pride and Prejudice* both characters are confined to a far more minimal description, which hardly ever allows the author's vision to appear at the surface of her exquisitely modulated sentences. Yet, as Virginia Woolf says, "Jane Austen is . . . a mistress of much deeper emotion than appears upon the surface. She stimulates us to supply what is not there,"[6] which may indeed include flesh, atmosphere, the color of Fanny Price's eyes. The technique is one practiced by an author commonly considered to be Austen's antipode. Ernest Hemingway knew that "you could omit anything if you knew that you omitted . . . and make people feel something more than they understood."[7] If this is so, the sensual details of Austen's world may emerge in a reader's mind along with the cadences of her ironically distanced prose, making the experience of reading Jane Austen a continual tension between sense and sensibility.

Fantasm and Fiction, unlike its predecessors, moves freely between the reader's visualization of a novel and the author's. This is not meant to imply that reader and author visualize exactly the same things. The author directs the reader's visualization: "literature consists of a steady stream of erased imperatives," according to Elaine Scarry,[8] imperatives that are often instructions to produce mental pictures. Yet no matter how detailed and precise those instructions may be, they are never comprehensive enough to override the individual's memory bank of images and associations. These play upon the author's dictated pictures, an obbligato of the unconscious, of memory and desire. In even the most fully realized fictional world there is a sense of this play, of figure and ground flickering in and out of each other in ways that I will consider at greater length in Chapter 3 of this book. Author and reader, then, share not a common visualization but a common *process* of visualization—for authors can be said, both in their writing and the focused imagining that precedes it, to be giving instruction to themselves quite as much as to their readers. The relation between author and reader is not a "communication" dynamic, with a visual content serving as its transmitted message. Instead, for both, the words on the page are the markers of a threshold state, framing and encouraging the production of mental images rather than communicating them as invariable and completed entities. Though readers may be possessed by an author's vision, as we will see in this book's first chapter, they are never wholly taken over—except in certain gothic narratives that exaggerate this aspect of reading.

The threshold state inhabited by both reader and author is the realm of the *fantasm*, a term I have taken from French psychoanalysis. There it can be applied to a whole range of visualizations. According to Herman Rapaport, in his survey of the concept, "Dreams, delusions, hallucinations, primal scenes, day dreams, imaginary objects, introjected symbols, fantasies, complexes, and phylogenetic imaginary constructions are all expressions of the *fantasme*."[9] These multiple aspects are united in posing a fundamental problem: "French psychoanalysts have become increasingly aware that the fantasm problematizes the relationships of word and image" (25). That problem is addressed by this book through an examination of various avatars of the fantasm. These unfold along a line that begins with the commonplace feeling of being engrossed by a good book, proceeds in a series of chapters that explore in more detail aspects of the reader's visualizing process, and concludes with a political challenge to, among other things, accepted notions of physical sight.

A *fantasm*, in English, is both a ghost and an image in the mind; and this overlap dominates my first chapter, "Possessed by Words." Historically, the power of a compelling work of fiction to take over its reader has been the subject of as much fear as fascination, for the images produced in the mind have disconcerting parallels to ghosts. Seeing them in their ghostly aspect may underscore the characteristics peculiar to mental images and their effects upon readers.

The source of those images cannot be in the words themselves: text is only a pretext for their release. It must be largely from the unconscious that such images are drawn, an unconscious that I argue, in my second chapter, is more visual than is currently assumed. The "Dream Book" of the chapter's title is any book seen in terms of dream; it is Freud's *Interpretation of Dreams*; and it is the botanical monograph that is the subject of one of Freud's most famous dreams. The chapter rereads all these dream books, and one other by Christa Wolf, in order to suggest that we re-envision the unconscious that clothes words with vision.

Any images arising out of the unconscious must nevertheless appear in conjunction with printed words on a page; and the relation between these words and these images is the subject of the book's third chapter. "Seeing the Forest for the Trees" begins with a cluster of tree metaphors in Eco, Calvino, Lacan, Irigaray, and Magritte, each suggesting a somewhat different take on words and the space between them. As those spaces become filled with visualizations, we have a shuttling between words and images that has philosophical implications for the ways that we construct the world, and our selves.

The modes of readerly visualization are themselves visualized in Chapter 4 by "Painters of Reading," those painters who have chosen the visualized text as their subject matter. If, as Merleau-Ponty asserted, painting's ultimate subject is visuality, that visuality extends beyond the physical world to the visual metamorphoses generated in the mind by print.

Every painting has a frame of one kind or another; and the paradoxes of the framing function play a role in the visions generated by fiction. Chapter 5, "Framing the Fantasm," examines the role of framing devices in producing illusions (Greenaway's film *Prospero's Books*), or hallucinations (Coleridge's poem "Kubla Khan"), or visions (Blake's drawing *The Inspiration of the Poet*).

In the last chapter, "A Politics of Visualization," I argue that the visualizing impetus of fantasy not only supplements, but can replace a normalizing vision. Throughout this book, I question, as others have done, the distinction between vision and visualization. Like all binaries, this one privileges one of its terms. Seeing is believing, according to popular wisdom; and visualizing is dismissed as mere fantasy. But fantasy, as any psychoanalyst knows, is a prime force in the subject's formation, as well as in what the subject sees—or believes is seen. Literary visualization has a certain congruency with such fundamental processes; it may even contribute to them if, as Freud asserts, "there is no 'indication of reality' in the unconscious, so that it is impossible to distinguish between truth and emotionally-charged fiction."[10]

This quick sketch may allow you to envision the shape of what is to come. With it, we have arrived at the threshold of the book proper. But before entering the book, it may be well to consider what that entry may sometimes involve, specifically in terms of visualization. Michel Foucault has argued that, in Flaubert's *The Temptation of St. Anthony*, the source of St. Anthony's terrifying visions is more likely to be reading than solitude in the wilderness: "The visionary experience arises from the black and white surface of printed signs, from the closed and dusty volume that opens with a flight of forgotten words."[11] So in the painting by Brueghel the Younger that impelled Flaubert to write *The Temptation*, the hermit kneels before an immense volume while all about him is a crowd of grotesques. The relation of the book to the fantasies is ambiguous. Is it a book of Holy Scripture, offering an escape from the forces of diabolic persecution? Or is it a magician's book, through which St. Anthony seeks to control these forces, or even through which he has summoned them? Doubtless the *kind* of book it is matters less than the *fact* of a book here, the effect of a book: "It may be . . . that these creatures of unnatural issue escaped from the book, from the gaps between the open pages or the blank spaces between the letters" (94).

Every book has these gaps, these blanks that are filled in reading, and thus has the potential for visionary experience. Christopher Collins, in *The Poetics of the Mind's Eye*, asserts that any imaginative work presents "a world in which figures, or fragments of figures, hover upon empty grounds, a bizarre world of floating synecdoches, of undulant Goyaesque phantoms. . . . Every poetic text simply by virtue of its medium simulates visionary events" (155). There is always, then, a certain risk in opening a book that leads us into a fictional world. For Mikhail Bakhtin the novel offers a lure: "We can experience these adventures, identify with these heroes; such novels almost become a substitute for our own lives. . . . And here we encounter the specific danger inherent in the novelistic zone of contact: we ourselves may actually enter the novel."[12] Entering a critical book like this one is a considerably less dangerous matter; but I would hate to think that there is no danger involved at all.

Possessed by Words

At one point in his novel *Absence*, Peter Handke describes a nocturnal act of reading:

The reader's eyes are narrow and curve at the corners, widening at the temples as though the letters and words, though only a few inches away, form a distant horizon. These eyes show that it is not he who is digesting the book but the book that is digesting him; little by little, he is passing into the book, until—his ears have visibly flattened—he vanishes into it and becomes all book. In the book it is broad daylight and a horseman is about to ford the Rio Grande.[1]

The impalpable act of reading here has a palpable effect—which is the paradoxical prelude to complete loss of the palpable, as the book ingests its reader. The flattened ears indicate a passage through what could be a birth canal as well as a gullet, but in either case is a passage out of the familiar self. Not merely absorbed in his book, this reader is absorbed *by* it, to the point of being taken over by an alien existence.

This takeover is like the one spoken of by Georges Poulet in "Criticism and the Experience of Interiority," the paper that he delivered at the 1966 Johns Hopkins conference on structuralism. What Poulet, in that paper, finds most extraordinary about the book is its passage from object to subject—to a subjectivity which is not that of the reader. The reader's response is indeed necessary to constitute it, but the subjectivity so constituted is that of an *other*. Otherness is no longer outside, in the material pages of the book; it constitutes itself "inside" the reading subject. However, at a certain point this ontology is turned inside out. Like Handke's reader, we are soon drawn inside the book; we think thoughts that are not our own and perceive, outside of those thoughts, the objects of the fictional world. But because that fictional world has come into being through the experience of interiority, the outside inhabited by these objects is also interior: they are what Poulet has called "subjectified objects." There is a liberating effect to this: "The greatest advantage of literature," Poulet asserts, "is that I am persuaded by it that I am free from my usual sense of incompatibility between my consciousness and its objects."[2] Yet there is an undertone of terror to this process as well: "So long as it is animated by this vital inbreathing inspired by the act of reading, a work of literature becomes *at the expense of the reader whose own life it suspends* a sort of human being. . . . It is a mind conscious of itself and constituting itself in me as the subject of its own objects" (62; emphasis mine).

Such language would justify us in seeing the act of reading as a kind of possession, a vampiric siphoning off of one's life blood to give vitality and movement to long-dead thoughts. Recognizing this possibility, Poulet immediately denies it:

If the work thinks itself in me, does this mean that, during a complete loss of consciousness on my part, another thinking entity invades me taking advantage of my unconsciousness in order to think itself without my being able to think it? Obviously not. (62–63)

Rather, a *common* consciousness is produced. The loss of consciousness is not complete; this saves readers from an ultimate ingestion and turns them into critics. There is of course some critical distance in any act of reading. Most readers will agree with Poulet that their subjectivity while reading is in a sort of divided trance: vigorous actions are received by us passively; there is a certain delay between our feelings and those of the book's subject; the book's events concern us greatly and at the same time have nothing to do with us. This separation from the experience of interiority is what defines criticism: "Aware of a certain gap, disclosing a feeling of identity, but of identity within difference, critical consciousness does not necessarily imply the total disappearance of the critic's mind in the mind to be criticized" (63). Other critics might resist Poulet on this point; Hans-Georg Gadamer, for instance, characterizes theory as "a true sharing, not something active, but something passive (pathos), namely being totally involved in and carried away by what one sees."[3]

Whether or not, like Poulet, we define the critical element as the opposite of this total involvement, as that which stands back to observe, to resist the total loss of consciousness, there is nevertheless always a degree of such loss. And that loss of one's own subjectivity is itself a possible subject of criticism, or of literature. I return then to the vampiric implications of Poulet's language earlier, implications corrected as excessive. Yet through that excess we may recuperate an element of reading that criticism (which has its own kinds of excesses) has generally held at bay.

Dracula's Library

Of course a few critics have considered, if only in passing, the notion of the text as vampire. Maggie Kilgour, for instance, has suggested that the literary past may, "like Dracula, prolong its life by feeding on the present."[4] This gives a sinister twist to the old idea of literary immortality, and to Poulet's notion that the subjectivity we partake of when we read is the author's. In Kilgour's view, it is we who are partaken of. This view appears in full vampiric dress in Carl Jacobi's 1933 story "Revelations in Black." Jacobi's story exemplifies what, to Poulet, is the most recognizable form of the reader's takeover by an alien subjectivity: "the sort of spell brought about by certain cheap kinds of reading, such as thrillers" (61). Jacobi's story is indeed a cheap thriller (original enough, nevertheless, to be included in the definitive *Penguin Book of Vampire Stories*), and as such casts a spell. But beyond this it is *about* the casting of a spell by a story.

In a dingy antique shop the unnamed narrator of Jacobi's story finds another story—a book to which he is attracted first because of the beauty of its black velvet binding, and then because of its cryptic contents, penned in an asylum by the shop owner's brother before his mysterious death. Unwilling to sell the book, the shop owner is at least willing to lend it. Upon opening it, the reader can make no sense of the book's opening paragraphs, but "something about the few sentences had cast an immediate spell of depression over me. The vague lines weighed upon my mind, and I felt myself slowly seized by a deep feeling of uneasiness."[5] The feeling impels him outside, through the streets of the city and to an abandoned mansion on its outskirts. Pushing open the gate, he sits for a while in the courtyard. Then, with a shock, he recognizes in the ornamental objects around him the originals of the book's cryptic references: he is in a sense inside the book. At this point he notices a beautiful veiled woman seated on a bench nearby. He excuses himself for trespassing, explaining that he took a stroll to relieve his mind from the bad effect of a book he was reading. "Books," the woman replies, "are powerful things. They can fetter one more than the walls of a prison" (290).

As the story continues, and as the narrator continues his nightly reading in the black book, he indeed becomes more and more the prisoner of his obsession; he is moving ever closer to the fate of his predecessor, the author of the book. Not until the black book's end is it revealed that the beautiful woman is a vampire. This revelation, according to "the old metaphysical law: evil shrinking in the face of truth" (298), confines vampiric power to its own grounds within the gate. However, the vampire has subverted the book's purpose by making its spell an extension of her own. Once this revelation has been made, the narrator frees himself through a double destruction: a stake through the heart, and the burning of the book. Neither the style of the telling nor the characterizations in "Revelations in Black" raise it above the usual "cheap thriller." The power of this story comes from its recognition and dramatization of, precisely, the power of a story.

A more sophisticated dramatization of the same paradigm of possession is Julio Cortázar's short (indeed short-short) story "Continuity of Parks." This story is about the reading of a novel—or rather (since the reading of the novel has already begun before the start of the story) it is about a certain crucial stage in reading, the stage described by Poulet. Indeed, Poulet's notion that reading produces a consciousness held in common by author and reader is reflected in the fact that the reader here can turn to his book only "after writing a letter giving his power of attorney and discussing a matter of joint ownership with the manager of his estate."[6] Obviously a man of power and wealth, the reader settles himself in a green velvet armchair overlooking the park of his estate. "The novel spread its glamour over him almost at once," we are told (64)—*glamour* here referring, as in fairy lore, to a spell that creates a visual illusion. The reader tastes "the almost perverse pleasure of disengaging himself line by line from the things around him . . . letting himself be absorbed to the point where the images settled down and took on color and movement" (64).

What emerges from this process is a passionate encounter in a mountain cabin between a man and a woman, fevered not by carnality but by the anticipation of their final task, soon to be fulfilled. She and he part at the cabin door to follow their respective parts of the plan. By now the "he" of Cortázar's story (the reader is identified only by this pronoun) has been absorbed into the "he" of the story he is reading. From a distanced sentence like "He was witness to the final encounter in the mountain cabin," we have moved to the intimacy of "The dagger warmed itself against his chest, and underneath liberty pounded." The elision through which this happens is as much psychological as grammatical, so that at this point the original "he" has vanished, become all book. The new "he" finds his way to the designated place and has no difficulty in passing the dogs, entering the grounds, the house.

The woman's words reached him over the thudding of blood in his ears: first a blue chamber, then a hall, then a carpeted stairway. At the top, two doors. No one in the first room, no one in the second. The door of the salon, and then, the knife in hand, the light from the great windows, the high back of an armchair covered in green velvet, the head of the man in the chair reading a novel. (65)

The story ends with this twist, a twist that is almost literal: the effect is that of a Möbius strip. Applied to reading, this image restores to the rather cozy-sounding concept of a "common consciousness" its latent terror. Instead of the neat division between witness and scene, there is only one side to this story. Just as there is a continuity of parks in their real and fictional versions, so there is a continuity of the subjectivity that "brings the story to life," literally. The fictional "he," having absorbed the reading "he," turns against him in a bid for final liberty. This time, the book will not be closed.

Spectralization

The uneasiness that underlies these visions of reading is an uneasiness about the very connection between reading and visions. It is not a new attitude. Terry Castle comments on the growing sense, in the late eighteenth and early nineteenth centuries, that reading was a "phantasmagorical process": "Medical writers . . . frequently warned that excessive reading—and especially reading books of a romantic or visionary nature—could send one into morbid hallucinatory states."[7] Cautions against such states reflect a deeper distrust of images in general, as Christopher Collins

has demonstrated in his *Reading the Written Image*, which traces iconophobia back to some of its earliest religious and social forms.

Yet, however much external images may generate distrust, internal
images do something more. "The problem we have with the images that are
produced in the 'dream of reason,'" Collins says, "is that these images are
not really *there* at all, but are *here*, haunting the very mind that observes
them."[8] This is another version of the elision between subject and object.
Moreover, Collins's terms allow us to hear an echo of Castle's. In her essay
on "The Spectralization of the Other in *The Mysteries of Udolpho*," Castle
detects in the gothic novel an internalization of the spirits of the departed.
Held in memory, images of the dead accompany the sensitive mourner
everywhere; no longer "there," they are constantly "here" in the way that
one's own subjectivity is. And, rather like the vampiric undead, they feed on
that subjectivity to body themselves forth. A phrase like Collins's "haunting the very mind that observes them" thus takes on a curious literality.
Ghosts, at the very moment that they have supposedly been banished by
Enlightenment rationalism, "retain their ambiguous grip on the human
imagination; they simply migrate into the space of the mind."[9]

The qualities of that space occupied by ghosts, whether in the mind
or out of it, play a significant part in Collins's theory of "groundless figures,"
evolved in a number of his writings.[10] Collins begins with the fact that
ghosts are often depicted as groundless, as hovering in space. This makes
them, he argues, like mental images—or, rather, like certain kinds of mental images. Using the Kantian distinction between productive and reproductive imagination, Collins analyzes the grounds of both, the grounds
against which their respective figures emerge. Reproductive imagination is
the mental recovery of stimuli already experienced; here, no matter what the
mind's eye focuses on, a periphery is implied and sensed beyond that focus.
In contrast, the images of the productive imagination—what the Greeks
called *phantasia*—have no such periphery. The focus may be expanded or
moved, but this is not sufficient to establish the sense of a preexistent
ground; the ground comes into existence only through our mental gaze.
What interests Collins is the effect of this curious groundlessness, which he
compares to the effect of featureless grounds in the external world—so-
called *ganzfelds* such as darkness, dense fog, or blank blue sky. These are
never perfectly blank: the eye projects various stimuli onto these fields, at
times even to the point of hallucination. Images may appear, figures against

the undifferentiated ground. For Collins, these factors explain much about the nature of visionary experiences, which commonly occur in solitude under conditions of sensory deprivation; they explain why the sky is the abode of spirits, and why ghosts float.

They also explain something about the mode of imaging cued by reading. The text's "productive" imagery emerges without peripheries: "Bound as we are to the sequence of the words, we can only imagine what the current words ask us to imagine."[11] In this sense our imagining is groundless, but it is so in a more physical sense as well: the blankness of the page is differentiated only by the print on the page, and that print, in generating figures, annihilates itself. Before standardized print, the chirographic peculiarities of the text could keep its objectivity to the fore, and could thus interfere with its passage into subjectivity. But standardized print acquired a kind of transparency. "In short," Collins concludes, "movable type not only made general literacy possible but created a new advance in phantasia, which we might term 'typographic imaging'" (9).

In these ways the book recedes as object, becomes an undifferentiated ground provoking the appearance of the mind's figures. The imagistic ghosts that "migrate into the space of the mind" with every vivid and participatory reading are produced, then, by processes related to those that caused ghosts to be seen in the first place. Most printed texts, Collins comments, "do not take advantage of this resemblance by thematizing the inner imagery of phantasia. Most in fact struggle against what I propose is the inherent tendency of the medium to evoke the phantasmagoric. . . . But those texts that do represent the envisioning of uncanny figures have the advantage of an exceedingly apt medium" (19). He is of course talking about ghost stories. These, as Elaine Scarry has pointed out, have a peculiar appeal that is related to the nature of the imagination's fantasms:

Why, when the lights go out and the storytelling begins, is the most compelling tale (or most convincing, most believable) a ghost story? Since most of us have no experience of ghosts in the material world, this should be the tale least easily believed. The answer is that the story instructs its readers to create an image whose own properties are second nature to the imagination: it instructs its hearers to depict in the mind something thin, dry, filmy, two-dimensional, and without solidity. Hence the imaginers' conviction: we at once realize, perhaps with amazement, that we are picturing, if not with vivacity, then with exquisite correctness, precisely the thing described. It is not hard to successfully imagine a ghost. What is hard is successfully imagining an object, any object, that does *not* look like a ghost.[12]

The Fantastic

While there is as yet no comprehensive theory of the ghost story, Tzvetan Todorov has given us a theory of "the fantastic," a theory that can further this book's aims: the genre's name is derived from the Greek *phantastikos*, whose verb form, *phantasein*, in late Greek comes to mean "to imagine, to have visions." Todorov does not pursue the implications of this. For him "the fantastic is that hesitation experienced by a person who knows only the laws of nature, confronting an apparently supernatural event."[13] Hesitation is the prime characteristic of the genre: if the supernatural is shown to be not just apparent but actual, the fantastic modulates into the marvelous; if the apparently supernatural act is explained by the laws of nature, then the fantastic becomes what Todorov for some reason calls "the uncanny." The fantastic hovers between, hesitating. This hesitation can be seen as connected to the disturbing epistemological questions raised by the status of mental visions. For as Todorov goes on to articulate his analysis of the fantastic he is also articulating many of the same problems raised by visionary images: Do they exist in the mind or outside of it? In what sense, if any, are they "real"? How do we distinguish between the creations of delusion or madness and those of normal perception? Thus, referring to what he calls, significantly, "themes of vision," (120) Todorov speaks of the "generating principle of all the themes collected in this first system: *the transition from mind to matter has become possible*" (114, emphasis in original). A bit later, he points out a further consequence of this principle: "the effacement of the limit between subject and object" (116). We are back to Poulet and the phenomenology of reading.

And indeed the problematic effects just spoken of are not to be separated from the effects of literature. For Todorov, "The fantastic is a kind of narrow but privileged terrain, starting from which we may draw certain hypotheses concerning literature in general. This," he adds, "remains to be verified, of course" (155). Nevertheless, it is almost axiomatic for Todorov that "what the fantastic speaks of is not qualitatively different from what literature in general speaks of, but that in doing so it proceeds at a different intensity" (93). Of what then does literature speak? Not only of its ostensible themes, but always already of its own self. To say this, of course, is to say no more than what New Criticism said long ago—but the accent may be different. If all literature partakes in the fantastic, as Todorov suggests, it becomes not a well-wrought urn but a floating fantom, unsettling in the extreme.

At one point in *The Fantastic*, Todorov is discussing the tendency for fantastic effects to arise out of the literalization of common figures of speech such as "to die laughing":

> If the fantastic constantly makes use of rhetorical figures, it is because it originates in them. The supernatural is born of language, it is both its consequence and its proof: not only do the devil and vampires exist only in words, but language alone enables us to conceive what is always absent: the supernatural. The supernatural thereby becomes a symbol of language, just as the figures of rhetoric do. (82)

The argument of this passage seems rather muddled to me. Quickly to raise some issues: Are all rhetorical figures (Spenser's "pretty epanorthosis and withal a paronomasia," for instance) equally supernatural in effect? Are the devil and vampires figures of speech, strictly speaking, or concepts? Doesn't conceiving what is absent (thus lending it a curious sort of presence) *itself* create an effect akin to the supernatural, even when it is not a supernatural entity that is being conceived? Yet despite my caviling about the way he gets where he is going, Todorov does present us with a provocative hypothesis: that "the supernatural . . . becomes a symbol of language." This remains to be verified, of course. And the verification is not found in this passage but in precipitation, as it were, throughout Todorov's book.

The same hesitation that characterizes the experience of a fantastic tale may characterize our experience of *any* tale. The language of literature both is and is not supernatural. On the one hand, its effects, especially its visionary effects, call up fantasmatic presences from another realm; we participate in their existence, and in proportion our own becomes more pale and wan: what is by all reasonable standards absent becomes present. On the other hand, we are never totally taken over, never lost in a book to the point of no return. We see the objective stimuli of page and print that give rise to these subjectivities, which may be viewed as more rationally hermeneutic than is implied by all this rhetoric of the supernatural, or the supernaturalness of rhetoric.

Most of the time, we forget the strangeness of reading. We do not hesitate over our experience—at least are not aware of doing so—but happily adapt to our amphibious existence as readers. That happiness may in part consist of the recovery of something lost, something we are not even consciously aware of having lost. Todorov quotes Jean Piaget on the child's perceptions: "Early in mental development, there exists no precise differentiation between the self and the external world" (118). What creates that differentiation, Todorov reminds us, "is the subject's accession to language. It is this accession which makes these particular features disappear in the first period of mental life: the absence of distinction between mind and matter, between subject and object" (145). We recognize in these primal features two already-noted features of the fantastic. Since these features have been part of everyone's normal experience, they compose a kind of natural supernaturalism. However, what is "natural" now is defined by our accession into language. Other modes of reality disappear, become derealized or repressed.

But the repressed returns, and one way it returns is through language, as Freud taught us. It does this not only through slips and fissures in language that betray its conscious surface, but through language that is consciously arranged to betray itself. Fiction, if only by the sheer fact of its fictionality, is such a conscious betrayal. The visionary worlds created in fiction do not have to succeed in taking us over completely; their liminal status (both here and not-here) is enough to remind us of language's reality-making properties. As we abandon our world to become absorbed by the book's world, we may vaguely sense that if words are capable of making a fictional reality appear, they are capable of making a "real" reality appear as well. To what degree, then, are both realities appearances? We hesitate, on this boundary line of language, between the natural and the supernatural. And if this is a disturbing state, it is also a familiar one: we have been there before, perhaps as infants, before the world became sorted out into subject and object, mind and matter.

Uncanny Reading

The fantastic nature of the reading act, then, its ability to call up fantasms, is at the same time familiar and unfamiliar—that is, it is *uncanny*. I am using this term now not in Todorov's rather inexplicable sense of "explicable" but in Freud's sense. Freud's idea of the uncanny, to be sure, arises out of a hesitation much like that which defines the fantastic: his starting point is Jentsch's notion that the uncanny is characterized by "*doubts* whether an apparently animate being is really alive; or conversely, whether a lifeless object might not be in fact animate."[14] Eventually, though, animism becomes the prime characteristic of Freud's uncanny: "We appear to attribute an 'uncanny' quality to impressions that seek to confirm the omnipotence of thoughts and the animistic mode of thinking in general, after we have reached a stage at which, in our *judgement*, we have abandoned such beliefs" (241n). At times Freud's ideas seem to anticipate Piaget's: the uncanny arises as "a regression to a time when the ego had not yet marked itself off sharply from the external world and from other people" (236). This regression unmakes repression—a repression that is reflected in the etymology of Freud's German term: "the *unheimlich* is what was once *heimisch*, familiar; the prefix 'un' is the token of repression" (245).

Yet the word, and consequently the concept, is not so neatly divided as that. Freud's own preliminary etymology reveals that what he calls "the antithetical sense of primal words," in his essay by that name, holds here. *Heimlich* means "homey, familiar"—but also "hidden, secret, dangerous." So, the last example Freud cites in his etymological study is from Klinger: "I feel like a man who walks in the night and believes in ghosts; every corner is *heimlich* and full of terrors for him" (226). Similarly, ghosts haunt another essay grounded in etymology, J. Hillis Miller's "The Critic as Host." In order to put into question facile notions about the relation of reader to text, Miller takes two paradigmatic terms, *host* and *guest*. He shows how these apparent antitheses exist on an etymological continuum and are transformed into each other. We may then replay in these terms certain problems raised in the beginning of this essay: Is the text the host and we the guests within it, feeding upon it? Or is the text a guest that we host, a bad guest, perhaps even a parasite that feeds on us? The hesitation that we may feel when asked to choose between these alternatives is rendered all the more disturbing by the etymology that floats between *guest* and *host*: the *ghost* whose uncanny manifestations are not perhaps so far removed from those we are familiar with in reading fiction.

Freud considers the literary application of his theory to be "a much more fertile province than the uncanny in real life, for it contains the whole of the latter and something more besides, something that cannot be found in real life" (249). He doesn't dwell on what that something is, but an earlier passage in the essay may offer us a clue: "An uncanny effect is often and easily produced when the distinction between imagination and reality is effaced, as when something that we have hitherto regarded as imaginary appears before us in reality, or when a symbol takes over the full functions of the thing it symbolizes, and so on."[15] In the example that follows, Freud gives us an idea of what he might mean by a symbol taking over the functions of the thing it symbolizes. He recalls a magazine story he once read,

a story about a young married couple who move into a furnished house in which there is a curiously shaped table with carvings of crocodiles on it. Towards evening an intolerable and very specific smell begins to pervade the house; they stumble over something in the dark; they seem to see a vague form gliding over the stairs— in short, we are given to understand that the presence of the table causes ghostly crocodiles to haunt the place, or that the wooden monsters come to life in the dark, or something of the sort. It was a naïve enough story, but the uncanny feeling it produced was quite remarkable.[16] (244–45)

The "symbol" here is an artistic depiction, a sign for the thing depicted. Other, less iconic signs are capable of the same effect. Not that words can "come to life" in the same way as the carved crocodiles do; but they can certainly cause ghostly crocodiles to haunt the reader's mind.

This immaterial haunting of the mind may also possess the body, taking over a different kind of function, a bodily function: pornographic novels cause sexual arousal, the plight of Clarissa causes tears to flow. Handke's reader is affected by his book with subtle physical changes—the eyes look as if they are viewing a distant horizon, not the proximate page. And any reader who has ever come under a story's spell is aware, the moment after closing the book, of the complex metabolic change throughout the body that we call our "reaction." If our full functions are not taken over, or are not fully taken over, this is all the more uncanny. We are *heimlich* in both its senses: we are cozy and domestic, ensconced in our comfortable chair; at the same time we are giving ourselves over to secret and perhaps dangerous forces without knowing, before we read, just what we are going to experience.

Still, the act of reading is so familiar that in order really to see it we must take on an unfamiliar perspective. We get just such a perspective in Gianni Celati's story "Readers of Books Are Ever More False." This is a tale for readers about nonreaders—nonreaders who learn to read, who nervously discover just what it means to read. For the young woman we observe here, print is at first boringly uniform after the glossy pictures of her movie magazines.

At the end of the winter, however, she noticed that the words and sentences she read in books—just because they made voices come into her mind—made an impression on her like ghost films.

Listening to all these allusions and insinuations about people and places and events and feelings, she began to have a feeling that she could not control and which put her on her guard about everything. They were like voices which emerged from a door opened on to the darkness. Alone in the house she listened to every slightest noise and peered at every shadow which looked a little unusual to her, because the words in a book had brought this trepidation upon her.[17]

And later: "She thought she made out in the printed lines something uncertain and indistinct—like a mute apparition against which the words moved restlessly" (88).

The ghosts or apparitions sensed by this young woman are manifestations of fiction's uncanny nature. "The direct figure of the uncanny is the Ghost," Hélène Cixous asserts in her reading of Freud's essay; for "the Ghost," she explains, "erases the limit which exists between two states."[18] Fiction does something similar, causing us to inhabit two states at the same time, to hesitate on the threshold between them without being able to demarcate clearly where one leaves off and the other begins. It is a psychoanalytic commonplace that an intense fantasy can seem more real and vivid than the blurred memory of ordinary days. Since this can also be true of the fantasmatically generated shapes of fiction, it is no wonder that Celati's young woman feels the trepidation she does. The bright, glossy surfaces of life are now no longer solid but evince a capacity to dissolve into other realms, images, and voices; what ensues is what Cixous calls "a phantomization of the present" (543). Fiction, she concludes, is the uncanny's double (548).

Banville's Ghosts

If this is so for readers (who are ever more false), it is no less so for the falsifying author. "To lie is to create," asserts the narrator of John Banville's novel *Ghosts*.[19] His creation is an island that has clear affinities with Prospero's, even resonating like his with strangely musical noises. As the novel begins, a boat has run aground and forced its occupants to wade to shore: "There are seven of them. Or better say, a half dozen or so, that gives more leeway," the narrator corrects himself. Such adjustments continue to be made throughout, allowing us to see the slippages of fiction: a straw boater is changed into a Panama; the author confesses to having lost track of which of the two boys is which; a sentence is abandoned midway and then rewritten. These evidences of the fictional lie are held in tension with fiction's creative power. Above all, the author's intention here, like that of Conrad in the preface to *The Nigger of the Narcissus*, is to make us *see*.

The opening pages of the novel are dense with references to seeing. One of the castaways is a photographer, continually raising her camera to her eye in order to capture the scene. The Professor, in his tower room atop the old house to which the little group makes its way, has a brass telescope mounted on his desk. But it is the dogsbody and (as it turns out) owner of the house who first sees the castaways: "Licht spied them from afar, with his keen sight" (4). Licht's name is an early index to the nature of a book whose scenes are shaped out of the amorphous and shifting moods of light. Light, as the castaways enter the house, is equated with Licht's sense of alarming new possibilities, those set in motion by the beginning of any fiction: "All he recalled for certain was the sense of being suddenly surrounded by something bright and overwhelming . . . [a] troupe of possibilities . . . tumbling and leaping invisibly about the hall. He saw himself in a dazzle of light, heroic and absurd, and the hallway might have been the pass at Roncesvalles" (12). The allusions to vision are so strong at the novel's opening that they suggest an optical reading of the first paragraph's conclusion. From the creating word that begins the book, and the characters—"Here they are"—we move to a brief description of the castaways' plight. What they want most of all is to be elsewhere. But "there is no elsewhere, for them. Only here in this little round" (3). "This little round" may ultimately be the field of vision: that of the reader, whose eyesight brings the characters into an existence no wider at any point than the words being read at the moment; and that of the author, who is visualizing the characters in a ghostly replication of the field of physical vision.[20]

As the novel progresses, another visual layer emerges, at first dimly and patchily, like pentimento. The "troupe" of castaways, and the possibilities they bring with them, become identified with the commedia troupes painted by Vaublin, a fictional version of Watteau. Vaublin is the subject of the Professor's opus, which is now turned over entirely to his assistant, our narrator. Watteau's *Embarkation for Cythera*, with its dying golden light and its curiously isolated figures making their way to the boat that will take them from the island, becomes superimposed on this island, these castaways. Likewise with the painting of *Gilles*, a version of Pierrot who, mocked by the rest of the troupe, stands with his arms hanging limply before him, a dullard who nevertheless possesses a tragic power. Evoked fleetingly at intervals in relation to the narrator, this image is eloquently described in the penultimate section of the book: an ekphrasis that functions rather like that peak moment in Noh theater where the actor abruptly stands stock-still, conveying in this way an emotion whose intensity is beyond word or gesture.

We assume that the description of *Gilles* has been written by the narrator, an art historian and a murderer. He has come to this island to assist the Professor after being paroled from prison, having served ten years of a life sentence for a monstrous crime, unmotivated as Raskolnikov's. The full story is given in the first volume of Banville's trilogy (*The Book of Evidence*, *Ghosts, Athena*). Here we are only hypothetically invited to consider the case of a man who becomes so obsessed with a Vaublin hanging in a great house that he steals it. Surprised by a maidservant, he forces her to accompany him, and then arbitrarily beats her to death with a hammer. Now the narrator quotes from his reading: "*I have an habitual feeling of my real life having passed and that I am leading a posthumous existence*" (25). He is in this sense a ghost. And indeed his presence in the narrative seems to slip curiously in and out of focus. At one point, having apparently settled himself with a cup of tea in the lounge, the narrator goes on to describe a long and intimate scene between characters who never betray any awareness of his presence. It seems that "though I am one of them, I am only a half figure, a figure half-seen, standing in the doorway, or sitting at a corner of the scrubbed pine table with a cracked mug at my elbow, and if they try to see me straight, or turn their heads too quickly, I am gone" (40). This ghostly mode of existence acquires flesh and presence for the first time in a later scene, when the two boys come upon the Professor's assistant burning trash, and a minimal conversation ensues. But of course these are words exchanged between ghosts: as the narrator's creations, the others in the story have a presence that is almost as insubstantial as his.

"Others?" the narrator questions himself; "Other: they are all one. The only one" (27). It becomes clear that this "one" is the murderer's victim, whose life was cut short by the hammer's blow. Now there is an overwhelming sense that restitution is demanded—restitution for an entire life, with all its rich multitude of details. "Details, details; pile them on" (8), the narrator advises himself, possibly echoing Ortega y Gasset in this regard.[21] To give a fully detailed life to these fictional others is, for the narrator, some kind of restitution for taking away the life of one. Writing becomes a kind of necromancy: "And so he waits for the rustle in the air, for the moment of sudden cold, for the soundless falling into step beside him that will announce the presence of the ghost that somehow he must conjure" (87).

It is not the dead as such this author seeks, nor yet the living: "No, no, something in between; some third thing" (29). The ghost, Cixous has said, exists between the two states of life and death; as does fiction, uncannily. The narrator's situation is like that of Castle's gothic heroines, whose mourning produces an interiorized fantom. And fiction itself, it can be argued, arises from such an imaginative act of mourning. Jacques Derrida has argued as much in *Memoires for Paul de Man*, a book dominated by the idea of mourning: "This mimetic interiorization is not fictive," he says—or not merely fictive: "it is the origin of fiction, of apocryphal figuration."[22] Consequently, Derrida is curiously insistent on the value and significance of the ghost:

The ghost, *le re-venant*, the survivor, appears only by means of figure or fiction, but its appearance is not nothing, nor is it a mere semblance. And this "synthesis as a phantom" enables us to recognize in the figure of the fantom the working of what Kant and Heidegger assign to the transcendental imagination and whose temporalizing schemes and power of synthesis are indeed "fantastic"—are, in Kant's phrase, those of an *art hidden* in the depths of the soul. (64)

The particular choice of words here suggests links between Derrida's concerns and mine in this chapter. Through the fantom there is a link to the fantastic, both as an epistemological state and as a microcosm of literature. Through the soul's "hidden" art that gives life to the art-object there is a link to the darker sense of the *heimlich* as secret. The *revenant* that is figure or fiction is related to the brains of gothic heroines, haunted by spirits coming back from the grave.

In Banville's novel, the *revenant* may also be a figure for the narrator, coming back from prison to a kind of afterlife. He seems to be neither alive nor dead, but "some third thing" between being and not being. And in a crucial passage we discover the degree to which this is true. The narrator speaks of how the days in his barren room would pass, one after another, until one day

I would look out the window and see that little band of castaways toiling up the road to the house and a door would open into another world. Oh, a little door, hardly high enough for me to squeeze through, but a door, all the same. And out there in that new place I would lose myself, would fade and become one of them, would be another person, not what I had been—or even, perhaps, would cease altogether. Not to be, not to be: the old cry. Or to be as they, rather: real and yet mere fancy, the necessary dreams of one lying on a narrow bed watching barred light move on a grey wall and imagining fields, oaks, gulls, moving figures, a peopled world. (221)

Between being and nonbeing, the narrator himself, we suddenly realize, exists as a fiction. His release from prison, his arrival at the island, his curious interactions with the castaways—all these are fantom imaginings of one who has never left his jail cell. To create is to lie. So we shift from Prospero's island to Robinson's—not only because of the solitude depicted in Defoe's fictional lie, but because of the truth behind the lie. Beginning with a quotation from Crusoe, Defoe explicates it in a surprising way:

When I was in my island kingdom, I had abundance of strange notions of my seeing apparitions, &c. all these reflections are just history of a state of forc'd confinement, which in my real history is represented by a confin'd retreat in an island; and 'tis as reasonable to represent one kind of imprisonment by another, as it is to represent any thing that really exists, by that which exists not.[23]

Defoe's time in Newgate prison, and the apparitions that came to him there, parallel the experience of the narrator—who has earlier alerted us by giving to the Professor the name Kreutznaer, Crusoe's family name before it became anglicized.

The narrator's manifest solitude now suggests that if there are not others but only one, that one is the narrator's own self. Yet that "self" is as ghostly as the shade of his victim. Self is the final fantom. So the narrator responds to Diderot on acting: "*The man who wishes to move the crowd must be an actor who impersonates himself.* Is that it, is it really it? Have I cracked it? And there I was all that time thinking that it was *others* I must imagine into life" (198–99). The insubstantiality and poignancy of this creative act, one's own life as one imagines it into existence, casts the whole of *Ghosts* in an elegiac light, like that which suffuses the world of *Embarkation for Cythera* or *Gilles*. Into this hushed world is set its little group of actors, or aristocrats, or lovers; it is "a world where they may live, however briefly, however tenuously, in the failing evening of the self, solitary and at the same time together somehow here in this place, dying as they may be and yet fixed forever in a luminous, unending instant" (231). This is not only a "phantomization of the present," but of presence itself, self-presence, the very idea of a self.

To read about this state is in some degree to enter it, readers becoming ever more false to their selves, whatever they imagine those selves to be. Now their imagining is placed at the service of an other, a fictional character that they become, though only up to a point. Neither one nor the other, readers are that third thing that hovers and hesitates, ghostlike, in a space *between*. Yet to be possessed in this way, to lose our self-possession, is not frightening, though it may be uncanny. It is most often a consummation devoutly to be wished. To fear that we are being absorbed by the author, as Poulet suggests at one point, is to forget that the author has enacted a similar process before, imagining characters to the point of being possessed by them. Peter Handke's novel *Across* concludes that "the storyteller is the threshold,"[24] conducting us through words to a liminal state. It is to another version of this liminal state that the next chapter will turn.

2

Dream Book

If the narrator of *Ghosts* is turning into fiction what he calls his "necessary dreams" (221), the same can be said of its author. "To me, writing fiction is like dreaming," Banville has confided.[1] He is not alone in thinking so: "I dream, therefore it gets written," Maurice Blanchot asserts (*Je rêve, donc cela s'écrit*).[2] And according to John Gardner "everyone who has ever seriously attempted a long fiction knows how remarkably similar writing is, in some respects, to dreaming."[3] This, he feels, is no less true for reading, which produces "a rich and vivid play in the mind. We read a few words at the beginning of the book or the particular story, and suddenly we find ourselves seeing not words on a page but a train moving through Russia, an old Italian crying, or a farmhouse battered by rain. . . . Fiction does its work by creating a dream in the reader's mind."[4] This dream is above all visual, another of the avatars of the fantasm.

Psychoanalytically, the fantasms of dream arise out of the contents of the unconscious. And this may be true as well for the fantasms of fiction. Even those whose experience of reading is less visual than Gardner's will have to admit that to read a work of fiction is not just to assimilate the words on the page. Rather it is to assimilate those words with something in the reader—a "something" that the reader, whose energies are otherwise occupied, draws on without close scrutiny. The play of the reader's unconscious manifests itself in language's tendency to deliver peripheral effects, such as oddly charged resonances between words, associations and their accompanying affects, and liminal imagery. Such effects arise out of what Freud called "the intricate network of our world of thought."[5] That network becomes reinforced and thickened at certain places when it is overlaid by a net of words; a fiction thus grows up in much the same way that a dream does—like, in Freud's image, "a mushroom out of its mycelium" (525).

If dreams are, as Freud asserted, the royal road into the unconscious (608), then to examine fiction under the aspect of dreaming is to raise again Freud's impossible question: What is the nature of the unconscious? For if the unconscious is, as it is often thought to be, fundamentally a linguistic construct, then it can scarcely be a very credible source for the images generated by reading. The most quoted formulation of this linguistic unconscious is Jacques Lacan's repeated assertion that the unconscious is structured as a language: "What the psychoanalytic experience discovers in the unconscious is the whole structure of language."[6] Lacan rereads Freud in this light, speculating that his thinking would have had a different shape if today's linguistic theories had been available to him. Without underplaying the importance of language in the unconscious, we may remind ourselves that the "whole structure of language" is not the whole of the unconscious—not in Freud, and not in Lacan. There is a visual element in Lacan's unconscious; and there is a notoriously uneasy tension between verbal and visual elements in Freud's. To pursue the agency of the image in the unconscious, I will begin, following Lacan's lead, by rereading Freud's key work, the work that is sometimes said to have discovered the unconscious, *The Interpretation of Dreams*.

Unbinding the Botanical Monograph

In many ways *The Interpretation of Dreams* is a monstrous book. It is enlarged in each of its editions up to the fifth; the sixth and seventh editions content themselves with new prefaces and a revised bibliography, and the eighth edition is once again enlarged. In the end the book has swollen to half again its original size, running 625 pages in the standard edition. These retrospective incorporations are paralleled by many instances, within the book, of material incorporated from the period during which the book was still being written. These could be described as prospective, revealing as they do anxieties over whether the book could actually *get* written. At one point Freud was stalled for over a year, before he could complete the book by writing the introductory survey of what everyone else had written on dreams. He attributed this delay to his reluctance to publish a book many of whose examples were drawn from his own dream life, with all that this might reveal about him. Analyzing a dream in which he found himself dissecting his own pelvis, Freud comments, "The dissection meant the self-analysis which I was carrying out, as it were, in the publication of this present book about dreams" (477). But "this present book" is in a sense never present: it is only about to be, or it is an interminable afterthought. At the same time its authoritative presence is terribly important to Freud, for upon this work he has staked all his claims to become the great man prophesied to his mother at his birth (192). A labyrinth of authorial anxieties and desires, of the paradoxical ways that writers turn into books, *The Interpretation of Dreams* at times reads as if its real author were Borges.

How, then, are we to get a handle on something as shifting and labyrinthine as Freud's dream book? Appropriately enough, through a dream about a book. The "dream of the botanical monograph," for all its brevity, is a condensation of fears and desires that reverberate throughout *The Interpretation of Dreams*. Ultimately, I would argue, it is *about* Freud's book, and not about what Freud needs to think it is about. The dream is given in the following words:

I had written a monograph on a certain plant. The book lay before me and I was at the moment turning over a folded coloured plate. Bound up in each copy there was a dried specimen of the plant, as though it had been taken from a herbarium. (169)

Freud really had written a monograph on a certain plant. The plant was the coca, and Freud's dissertation had recommended the use of cocaine as an anesthetic—though the actual use of cocaine in this way, and the credit for its success, was left to another. In this dream, Freud tells us, "the central point of the dream-content was obviously the element 'botanical'" (305). Accordingly, he proceeds to trace out a complex network of botanical associations and puns. These include an encounter the day before with a Professor *Gärtner* ("gardener") and his wife, whom he had complimented on her *blooming* looks. Just before this encounter a patient named *Flora* had been mentioned in the course of a wide-ranging conversation on professional matters with Freud's colleague Dr. Königstein. It is this conversation, or rather the concerns raised by it, that is indicated by the botanical allusions: "All of these trains of thought, when they were further pursued, led ultimately to one or other of the many ramifications of my conversation with Dr. Königstein" (173). The dream thoughts, Freud says, "were concerned with the complications and conflicts arising between colleagues from their professional obligations, and further with the charge that I was in the habit of sacrificing too much for the sake of my hobbies" (305). We may be excused, I hope, for not immediately seeing the connection between these perfectly conscious daylight concerns and the form found for them by the unconscious. The connection, Freud asserts, lies in the general self-justification with which he meets reproaches of a professional kind: he may do as he sees fit because "After all, I'm the man who wrote the valuable and memorable paper (on cocaine)" (173). This, at any rate, is a first explanation of the dream.

Freud himself indicates that another and very different reading is possible, discovered through the associations evoked in him by the monograph's folded plate. He recalls that when he was five his father gave to him and his younger sister Anna a book with colored plates in it, which they were allowed to destroy. He seems to remember them pulling it to pieces, leaf by leaf, "like an artichoke," which Freud is in the habit of referring to, jokingly, as his "favorite flower." On returning to the dream of the botanical monograph, twenty pages on in his book, he assures his readers that "the ultimate meaning of the dream, which I have not disclosed, is intimately related to the meaning of the childhood scene" (191). Alexander Grinstein, in his book *On Sigmund Freud's Dreams*, feels that this incident is rather unlikely to have occurred, given the strict child-rearing practices of the Freud family. Grinstein finds the meaning to be allusive rather than factual, reminding us that in the slang of that day "pulling out" a piece referred to masturbation.[7] Elizabeth Grosz also questions the factuality of this incident, which she sees as a screen memory for another scene. When Freud was five his father gave him a Bible, saying it was the dearest thing in the world to him "except his spouse." This implied equivalence between the book and the mother's body is at the root of Freud's Oedipal desire both to read books and to write them.[8]

All of these interpretations spread their net wide—wider than my summary of them has indicated. I have only foregrounded the most crucial elements, which is of course what interpretations always do. Let us now consider what has been left out. Only once, among Freud's wide-ranging associations, are we given a source for the dream of the botanical monograph that almost directly corresponds to Freud's description of it:

I had had a letter from my friend [Fliess] in Berlin the day before in which he had shown his power of visualization: 'I am very much occupied with your dreambook. *I see it lying finished before me and I see myself turning over its pages'*. How much I envied him his gift as a seer! If only *I* could have seen it lying finished before me! (172; emphasis in original)

This last sentence is obviously a wish, and if we cannot account for all the particular terms of its fulfillment, it is still clear that fulfillment is what the dream has provided. However, when he comes to summarize the main sources of his dream, Freud (along with his interpreters) forgets this one entirely. His summary lists only two sources: an actual monograph on *The Genus Cyclamen*, which Freud had glimpsed in a shop window the previous morning; and the conversation with Dr. Königstein. The first source accounts for the fact that Freud's dream book takes the guise of a botanical monograph. The second source, I would argue, deflects attention from inchoate anxieties underlying the just-drafted dream book. The correspondence with Fliess would place this dream a few days before March 10, 1898, at which point the manuscript had just been completed, with the exception of the first chapter; after this, work came to a standstill until the end of May 1899. If the dream reflects certain paralyzing problems, the interpretation substitutes a conscious professional concern that has the virtue of being familiar: "a matter which never fails to excite my feelings whenever it is raised" (171).

Among the anxieties which are both betrayed and overcome by the dream's wishful completion of the book, we must include an anxiety about visualization. For in Freud's account of Fliess's letter *two* wishes are expressed: Freud wishes to see his book lying finished before him and, quite simply, he wishes to *see*. He envies Fliess his gift of visualization, a gift whose lack he detects even in his dreams. "My dreams are in general less rich in sensory elements than I am led to believe is the case in other people," Freud admits just before describing an exception to this rule, a dream whose rich coloration was "traceable to a visual stimulus" (547). Because Freud is not naturally prone to visualization in his waking life any more than in his dream life, he is led to a technique of dream analysis that emphasizes the verbal.

Freud's practice is to write down the dream and then to analyze the *written account*: "I have followed the fundamental rule of reporting a dream in the words which occurred to me as I was writing it down. The wording chosen is itself part of what is represented by the dream" (455). Now, it is not my intention to deny the manifold links between the word and the unconscious; in fact, I would maintain that if there were no such links, reading—of dreams, of fictions—could scarcely take place at all. But if language is linked to the unconscious, it is not for that reason the only way in, the royal road. Other paths are possible, and to depend exclusively on the way of words is to close these off. Insofar as the verbal is one of the aspects of the preconscious it does border the unconscious. But it can just as easily face in the other direction, the direction of something other than the dream's actual mode: the direction of control, of eloquent explications that may be at bottom only evasions.

An example is Freud's dream of being assigned an anatomical task: "STRANGELY ENOUGH, it related to a dissection of the lower part of my own body" (452). The first two words, set in capitals by Freud, are "a clear expression of astonishment" as the dream begins. Yet the rest of the sentence is considerably less astonished: "my pelvis and legs, which I saw before me as though in the dissecting-room, but without noticing their absence in myself and also without a trace of any gruesome feeling." In the dream's analysis, the words, not the felt experience, recall a discussion he had had earlier about Rider Haggard's *She*, which he had called a "strange" book. While the book's contents can be related to certain images in the dream, it is surely significant that we are pivoted toward a conscious literary assessment by way of a word that had no actual presence in the dream. Freud, in fact, often equates the dream and the words that sum it up; in another instance he writes "'overcome by strange emotions' were the words used in the dream itself" (480). Here he confuses the experienced dream with its written summary, which is moreover clearly inadequate to convey the actual emotions felt—indeed in a sense contradicts them. For in both instances the retrospective reference to "strangeness" arises out of a conscious base of judgment that is quite different from the feeling of the dream state.

We remember that the talking cure is meant to bring the contents of the unconscious into the preconscious, where words are capable of "binding" them. It is not really surprising, then, that words are privileged over other modes in which dreams take place, especially the visual. Nowhere is this more evident than in Freud's use of the rebus. Images, which Freud freely admits are the basic medium of dreams, cannot be taken on their own terms but must be translated into language, as are certain picture puzzles. In these puzzles a picture viewed as a whole seems nonsensical, but if the various pictorial elements are translated piece by piece (often in punning ways) into verbal equivalents, the pieces of the picture become words in a sentence, and the puzzle is solved. A dream is such a rebus, Freud claims, and must be read accordingly. "There is no need to be astonished at the part played by words in dream-formation," he assures us. "Words, since they are the nodal points of numerous ideas, may be regarded as predestined to ambiguity; and [dreams] make unashamed use of the advantages thus offered by words for purposes of condensation and disguise" (340–41).

Images, however, offer the same advantages; ambiguity is a common characteristic of the dream image, as in Wordsworth's dream of the Arab:

> He, to my fancy, had become the Knight
> Whose tale Cervantes tells, yet not the Knight,
> But was an Arab of the desert too;
> Of these was neither, and was both at once.[9]

Images are even capable of a kind of pun, as demonstrated by Salvador Dali's recurrent practice (influenced, incidentally, by Lacan's studies of paranoia), or the well-known rabbit-duck diagram from the pages of Freud's beloved *Fliegende Blätter*.

If I am troubled by Freud's tendency to slip from a visual to a verbal signifier, the relation between them seems to have given Freud some trouble too. The problem is one of translation, and the direction in which it moves. "The dream-content," Freud says, "seems like a transcript of the dream-thoughts into another mode of expression, whose characters and syntactic laws it is our business to discover by comparing the original and the translation" (277). But what is this original? In the rebus model, images are translated back into the words of the message. Yet underlying those words is their origin in images; in Freud's 1916 lecture "The Dreamwork" he tells us, "Our thoughts originally arose from sensory images. . . . Their first material and their preliminary stages were sense impressions, or, more properly, mnemic images of such impressions. Only later were words attached to them and the words in turn linked up into thoughts."[10] Words are bracketed by images here, arising out of images and then being translated back into different images by the dream-work. And "thoughts" occupy a no less ambiguous position, elicited first by images that become words and then, as "dream thoughts," expressed in words that become the images of rebus. The whole system is a complex detour that begins and ends in image, not without altering the image in the process.

Now let us look again at the dream of the botanical monograph. Its time sense is interesting: it depicts a specific moment ("*I was at the moment turning over a folded coloured plate*"); yet it shows a knowledge of the book's nature that extends beyond that moment ("*Bound up in each copy there was a dried specimen of the plant.*"). If the moment of the dream were extended, the first thing to be revealed would be that which is found upon turning over or unfolding the plate—that is, the illustration. But where we would expect a description of the illustration, we get a reference to the dried specimen, which is surely not to be found within this "folded coloured plate"—or, at least, not logically. The syntactic laws of the dreamwork, however, are not those of the daylight world. Despite, or along with, the implication that the specimen is bound up somewhere else in the copy, the juxtaposition here suggests that the dried specimen is what is seen as the colored plate is unfolded, just as it is the next thing to be unfolded by the words.

In these ways, the botanical monograph enacts a problem that it can never unfold completely, that of representation in dreams. Three modes of representation are involved. Like the book Freud had already written on cocaine, and the one he was writing on dreams, this book's prime medium must be verbal. Assuming or ignoring the verbal element here, attention is focused on the pictorial element, incipient but not fully revealed. And finally, occupying a peculiarly unfixed position in the dream experience, there is the actual thing, in a desiccated version of its materiality (it surely has some significance that "Flora" is the name of one of Freud's real patients, here flattened between the pages of a book).[11] These three modes of representing the subject of the monograph, with the peculiarities that we have noted, echo the shifting relationships between "word," "image," and "thought" in the passage from the "Dreamwork" lecture. I am not suggesting a direct correspondence between these two instances—only that a tremor of uncertainty about questions of representation underlies in each instance Freud's supposed self-justification. While repeatedly touching upon questions of representation, Freud swerves away from any rigorous challenge to his logocentric assumptions. The chapter entitled "The Means of

Representation in Dreams," which one would expect to tackle these questions on their largest scale, is devoted to a refinement of his method, explaining how abstract grammatical relations may be represented in dreams.

While hinting at problems of representation, *The Interpretation of Dreams* closes the book on them; like the botanical monograph, it *contains* these problems in two senses. First, in the sense that the problems are controlled, bound between covers and in the form of words; second, in the sense that the problems continue to reverberate within the book, unadmitted and unresolved. This lack of resolution puts the writer into a kind of double bind involving, in both directions, the unbinding of his words. There is a natural anxiety lest the entire fabric of the book be unbound by a flaw in its final form that might betray itself to a critical reader. That reader must be preempted by the author; any objections must be anticipated and overcome. But one cannot be sure where this process will stop: it could lead to the overwhelming task of reconceiving and rewriting the whole book. In fulfilling a wish that the book be seen as finished, the dream of the botanical monograph overcomes such anxieties, which cannot afford to be too closely defined. At the same time, the dream implies these anxieties, for one does not wish for what one already has.

Only a couple of pages before the end of his book, Freud presents two final examples. One of these is a standard betrayal of sexual impulses through the words chosen by the patient. But the second example is that of a fourteen-year-old boy, whose analysis, atypically, has proceeded by way of his mental *pictures*. "I began the treatment by assuring him that if he shut his eyes he would see pictures or have ideas, which he was then to communicate to me. He replied in pictures" (618). The analysis proceeds by way of these pictures, which are nowhere treated as rebuses, and it concludes successfully: "*In this case* long-repressed memories and derivatives from them which had remained unconscious slipped into consciousness by a roundabout path in the form of apparently meaningless pictures" (619; emphasis mine). But mental pictures do not only have a meaning, in this case; they are themselves a mode of meaning, a language of the unconscious.

Lacanian Poetics

These mental pictures are a language of the unconscious in Lacan's sense, if we understand that sense properly. "I have never said that the unconscious was an assembly of words," Lacan told the audience of his Johns Hopkins talk, "but that the unconscious is precisely structured."[12] The dictum that the unconscious is structured as a language must be understood, then, to mean that it is structured *in the way* that a language is structured: indeed, Lacan goes on to say that "'structured' and 'as a language' for me mean exactly the same thing."[13] This is not to say that language, in its usual sense, is not among the structuring principles of the unconscious. But it is one among various modes of structuration.

The Lacanian unconscious is everything Other than the infant, whose biological helplessness renders it a receptive object of structuring stimuli: the language in which it is bathed, the images presented to the child's gaze and the experience of the gaze itself, apprehensions of solidity and space. Of such as these are made up the infant's fundamental structurations. The sense of "self" that emerges from this influx of Otherness is referred to as the *moi*—the term's grammatical case emphasizing its position as object of Otherness. The *moi*'s structuring codes underlie the developments that follow, leading to the *je*, or speaking subject. Language as spoken by the *je* functions in a way that is different from its function as an aspect of the unconsciousness's structuration, even before coherent articulation is possible.[14] With the child's arrival at the symbolic stage, language becomes a tool of consciousness for controlling and containing the unconscious—which nevertheless subverts language in moments of incoherence such as the classic Freudian slip. In contrast, language as experienced by the *moi* might fall under Freud's category of *Wahrnehmungszeichen*—"perception marks" or "signifying marks"—whose importance lies not so much in what they signify as in the very *idea* of signification as a principle. Spoken language is only one of the possible *Wahrnehmungszeichen* that obtrude upon the infant, and it is intermixed with other modes of marking by the Other.

Language in the symbolic stage remains capable of evoking those primordial intermixings; and Ellie Ragland-Sullivan's "Prolegomena to a Lacanian Poetics" is one example of how this might be so. At the end of her essay, Ragland-Sullivan sums up her project:

A Lacanian poetics would claim that the purpose of reading and writing literary texts is to evoke a shadow meaning network whose structures, messages and effects control our lives, but whose truths are evasive. These evocations infer a dream-like quality to images, a Real power to words, and a concrete materiality to language which vibrate all the way back to a representational memory bank, starting with sensory impressions of the mother's body, and a haunting sensation of disembodied gazes and voices.[15]

Literature is thus a privileged use of language in such a way as to evoke the Other of the unconscious. This is not to say that literature gives us direct access to that unconscious. Rather its rhetorical effects take us past grammar to structuring dynamics that are parallel to those of the unconscious: metaphor and metonymy are cognate with condensation and displacement; repetition echoes the process by which a *moi* is constituted; words flicker with images and emotions in the same way that "in our unconscious, linguistic elements are tied to visual elements, to impressions and effects."[16] A literary text does not reveal to us a specific truth dug up from our unconscious. Rather it evokes the truth *of* the unconscious, of the modes that have made us without our knowing it. Nor can we know them now, except in an allusive dynamics like that of dreams.

In Lacan as in Freud, dreams are a way into the unconscious, even if they are not to be equated with the unconscious itself. If that unconscious is visual as well as verbal, it may at first seem puzzling when Lacan states that "our position in the dream is profoundly that of someone who does not see."[17] Seeing, here, means an active and conscious gaze, in contrast to the vision to which the subject is subjected in dreams—and is in fact always subjected, with or beneath its own conscious gaze: "In the so-called waking state, there is an elision of the gaze, and an elision of the fact that not only does it look, *it* also *shows*. In the field of the dream, on the other hand, what characterizes the images is that *it shows*" (75). What is this "it" that shows? It may be associated with the *es* of Freud's famous pronouncement *Wo es war, soll Ich werden*, sometimes mistranslated as a small narrative of mastery: Where id was, there ego shall be. In Lacan's reading the movement is quite the opposite. Ego is necessarily entrammeled in something less categorizable than "id": an impersonal *it* that is Other than the constructed subject. In dreams the Other shows not itself but images. And these images are not representations of some stable entity behind them; rather their structuring mechanism reveals something of the structuring forces operating upon, even constituting, the human subject at the unconscious level. "Lacan," Ragland-Sullivan states, "inferred an underside to literary language (and its interpretations) which is neither grammatical, logical, or rational, but is proof of a knowledge which, although enigmatic and elusive, is palpable and Real."[18] Consequently, she concludes, "a Lacanian poetics would argue that literary texts align themselves with dreams," as well as with other manifestations of a Real beyond consciousness and convention.

Hypnagogia

One markedly visual manifestation of such a Real is the phenomenon known as *hypnagogia*—the quasi-hallucinatory images that may arise in the state immediately prior to sleep. Pouring into the chink between waking and sleeping, these images are so rich, so volatile, that one is tempted to think of them as a stream of unconsciousness. Certainly they seem generated by something other than the perceiver, who can watch images suspended before the closed eyes, changing rapidly according to a logic of their own. The perceiver is awake throughout—though the progression of images may often lead into a dream proper, as sleep overcomes the subject. This phenomenon, which occurs occasionally in most people (perhaps all people, if they were alert enough to notice it), is essentially a visual one; however, other forms, such as the audial, are occasionally experienced.[19] In *Speak, Memory*, Vladimir Nabokov lists "hypnagogic mirages" among the "mild hallucinations" to which he is prone. He describes

the slow, steady development of the visions that pass before my closed eyes. They come and go, without the drowsy observer's participation, but are essentially different from dream pictures for he is still master of his senses. They are often grotesque. I am pestered by roguish profiles, by some coarse-featured and florid dwarf with a swelling nostril or ear. At other times, however, my phantasms take on a rather soothing *flou* quality, and then I see—projected, as it were, upon the inside of the eyelid—gray figures walking between beehives, or small black parrots gradually vanishing among mountain snows, or a mauve remoteness melting beyond moving masts.[20]

Freud speaks of hypnagogia for only two pages of *The Interpretation of Dreams*, in the introductory survey of the literature on dreaming. Hypnagogia is presented as an example of the somatic stimulus to dream images—specifically, the origins of such images in retinal excitations. This theory, held by Henri Bergson among others, is explicitly denied by Nabokov, who distinguishes his hypnagogic images from "the so-called *muscae volitantes*–shadows cast upon the retinal rods by motes in the vit-

reous humor, which are seen as transparent threads drifting across the visual field" (34). But Freud has something to gain by classifying hypnagogic
images among the external stimuli of dreams. He avoids the problem of
having to find a place for the hypnagogic state in the layered topography of
mental life which he has modeled in the section on regression near the end
of his book (but, of course, before the first chapter was written). The most
logical place to locate the hypnagogic state would be the preconscious, situated between conscious and unconscious and thus cognate to hypnagogia's position between sleeping and waking. However, this would entail
significant revision of Freud's idea of the preconscious state as the modifying or "critical agency" that screens the unconscious from consciousness.
Moreover, Freud would have to reconsider his argument that dreams are
created from a regression to original perceptions, in clear distinction from
the waking state: "In the waking state . . . this backward movement never
extends beyond the mnemic images; it does not succeed in producing a
hallucinatory revival of the *perceptual* images" (543). But hallucinatory images are exactly what are produced in hypnagogia, and these appear before
the eyes (usually closed, but sometimes open) of a subject who knows himself to be awake. All of these problems are sidestepped by the simple expe-
dient of acceding to the common wisdom of Freud's day, that hypnagogic
images arise from physical rather than psychical causes.

Maneuvers like these would no doubt exacerbate Nabokov's habitual
grumpiness about "the Viennese quack," as he called him, which seems to
have been unremitting: every morning Nabokov would review his dreams
of the night before and take "gleeful pleasure" in explicating them with no
reference whatsoever to Freudian theory, that "charlatanic and satanic non-
sense."[21] The biggest crime of Freudian theory, for Nabokov, may have
been its tendency to replace the actual dream images with their "interpretation"—an interpretation being, as Susan Sontag long ago pointed out, always the translation of an experience into a paradigm that is not the same
thing as that experience. This is the common activity of criticism. But as
an artist, Nabokov observed, images were more important to him than
ideas (7).

By attacking Freud, then, Nabokov is defending his individual mode
of creativity—and possibly that of others. In his study of hypnagogia, Andreas Mavromatis sees a link between hypnagogic states and creativity: in
both cases "there is present what might be called an activity of *imaginal per-*

ception, that is, an experience of vivid, lifelike imagery" (195). His argument is that ideas compose themselves through such imagery before the flash of insight is translated into words and embedded in logic. Moreover, the terrain on which this activity takes place often sounds much like that of a hypnagogic state. Virginia Woolf, for instance, describes the activity of the writer in this way: "After a hard day's work, trudging around, seeing all he can, feeling all he can, taking in the book of his mind innumerable notes, the writer becomes—if he can—unconscious. In fact, his under-mind works at top speed while his upper-mind drowses. Then after a pause the veil lifts; and there is the thing—the thing that he wants to write about—simplified, composed."[22] While the drowsiness here cannot be taken literally, creative minds as diverse as Thomas Edison and Salvador Dali have indeed set themselves to drowse when they wanted to utilize the hypnagogic state. In order to keep themselves from lapping over into actual sleep, they dispose themselves in such a way that the body's relaxation triggers a stimulus to pull them back from sleep with presleep images intact—Edison's hands, for instance, would let drop a set of iron balls into a pan below.

The apprehension of "the thing that he wants to write about" has most famously been described by Coleridge in his preface to "Kubla Khan"; he tells us that "all the images rose up before him as *things*, with a parallel production of the correspondent expressions." This took place in "a profound sleep, at least of the external senses." And one critic, Arthur Koestler, has seen the nature of this experience to be hypnagogic.[23] But Coleridge's creative state not only generates words; it is generated by them, specifically by a sentence from *Purchas's Pilgrimage*, in ways that we will examine closely in another chapter. Here let us take the poem as an indication that hypnagogic creativity can be an aspect of not only the writer's experience but also the reader's. Both experiences, of course, are liminal states. Indeed, the psyche of a reader is so curiously disseminated that to speak of "reader response" is deceptive, implying as it does an autonomous subject answering to something outside of itself. The state involved is much more closely analogous to Mavromatis's description of hypnagogia:

In hypnagogia a person may gradually relinquish the attitude of [separative] contemplation and, by being absorbed in imaginal activities, become 'fascinated'. . . . Autosuggestibility and psychological incorporability or internalization of the [imaginal] environment (subjectification of the object) are thus attentional attributes of that aspect of receptivity which is operational in hypnagogia. (70)

The somewhat clotted terms in which Mavromatis describes hypnagogia can also be found in writings about the reader's psychological state.

First, take the parenthetical reference to "subjectification of the object." We find almost the same phrasing in Poulet's essay "Criticism and the Experience of Interiority":

Doubtless what I glimpse through the words, are mental forms not divested of an appearance of objectivity. But they do not seem to be of another nature than my mind which thinks them. They are objects, but subjectified objects. In short, since everything has become part of my mind thanks to the intervention of language, the opposition between the subject and its objects has been considerably attenuated.[24]

This sounds comforting. Maurice Blanchot, however, finds more disturbing qualities in the state of *fascination*, which he conceives of as "passion for the image."[25] In fascination we never close the distance between ourselves and the "thing." All our negotiations are with the image, which may allude to the thing, but is always other than it, and thus alludes ultimately to Otherness. "To write," Blanchot writes, "is to let fascination rule language. It is to stay in touch, through language, in language, with the absolute milieu where the thing becomes image again, where the image, instead of alluding to some particular feature, becomes an allusion to the featureless."[26] That "featureless" Other may be akin to the unspecified ground out of which arise the fluctuating figures of Nabokov's hypnagogia. In saying this I do not intend to equate Mavromatis's "fascination" and Blanchot's, any more than I am flatly equating the reading trance to the hypnagogic state.[27] Yet certain features of reading and hypnagogia are analogous, suggesting that both may be ways into the unconscious, an unconscious that is visual as well as verbal.

Envisioning Cassandra

In one of the essays published with Christa Wolf's *Cassandra* and which describe the novel's genesis, Wolf describes a hypnagogic experience which is the prolongation of her bedtime reading. Lying in her bunk during a night voyage to Crete, she reads "a bloody history from the partisan period" given her by its author. That author is also a translator of Aeschylus, whose *Oresteia* Wolf began reading at the start of her trip to Greece.

She has increasingly become haunted by Cassandra and her world. Now, as she puts away the book and drifts toward sleep, the ancient and modern worlds combine in a single vision:

Just at the last I saw the facial expression of this partisan, a young man with dark hair and beard, whose head—such was the archaic language in which my speaking consciousness expressed itself in my sleep—suddenly floated upon the waters; I do not know how else to say it. Somewhere in the last few days I must have come across the singing head of Orpheus. A youthful head, which I knew belonged to a man named Aeneas, was floating on smooth, oily water, surrounded by the petals of water lilies and other verdure. He was looking at me, painfully demanding. And I knew of course, without expressly having to think it, that this Aeneas was also the young partisan whose assuredly ghastly end I had not wanted to know. Knew that these two men, separated by more than three thousand years, had as if casually been imprinted with the same expression, the expression of the losers who do not give up, who know: they will lose again and again, and again and again will not give up, and that is no accident, no mistake or mishap, but it is meant to be that way. The thing that no one wants to believe—that head floating on the water believed and knew, and that was the most dreadful shame, the real crying shame, and it was the greatest delight: Aeneas.[28]

Another example of hypnagogia occurs at the close of Wolf's story "Tuesday, September 27":

I can still observe the first transitions to the pictures one sees before falling asleep; a street appears leading to that landscape I know so well without ever having seen it: the hill with the old tree, the softly inclined slope up to a stream, meadowland, and the forest at the horizon. That one can't really experience the seconds before falling asleep—otherwise one wouldn't fall asleep—I will forever regret.[29]

Why "regret"? Because these images, as with the apprehension of Aeneas above, are seen by Wolf as the direct source of her creativity, and this is so whether hypnagogia leads into the dream proper (as in the second example) or comes out of a reading experience. Image is both a source of art and a product of it.

So it is with the image of Cassandra, glimpsed within the words of Aeschylus. When she reaches a certain point in *The Oresteia*, Wolf immediately falls under Cassandra's power:

I witnessed how a panic rapture spread through me, how it mounted and reached its pinnacle when a voice began to speak:

Aiee! Aieeeee!
Apollo! Apollo!

Cassandra. I saw her at once. She, the captive, took me captive; herself made an object by others, she took possession of me. (*Cassandra*, 144)

Throughout the protracted plane trip and the tour of Greece, Cassandra's burgeoning presence provided counterpoint or commentary for each day's events. What is seen in contemporary tourism was juxtaposed with another kind of seeing, generated by literature ("I saw her at once"), though not invariably: "Cassandra outside the gates of Mycenae (I cannot visualize it: the Lion Gate? The gates of the palace inside the fortified wall?)" (149). As Wolf reads in the midst of a crowded boarding area, "the lines of Aeschylus dangle before my eyes like a coarse netting through whose wide meshes I see a figure stir" (148). The simile of the net here is a curious one. Alluding to the merely approximate capacity of words to capture life, it also alludes to a specific scene of capture: the ensnaring of Agamemnon in a net before he is killed. Is Cassandra likewise murderously ensnared? Yes, in the first place because Aeschylus reads her wrong and thus writes her wrong; coming to Cassandra's declaration that she mourns Agamemnon's fate, Wolf knows that it is a "mistake" (the quotation marks are hers). In her preface to the four essays that accompany *Cassandra,* Wolf more generally observes, "There is and there can be no poetics which prevents the living experience of countless perceiving subjects from being killed and buried in art objects. . . . So, does this mean that art objects ('works') are products of the alienation of our culture, whose other finished products are produced for self-annihilation? . . . My overall concern," she concludes, "is the sinister effects of alienation, in aesthetics, in art, as well as elsewhere" (142).

In reading Aeschylus's Cassandra, Wolf begins to function as a kind of "alienist"; it becomes her project to bring Cassandra back to herself. By seeing her fully, more fully than Aeschylus allows, she wishes to free Cassandra from a certain idea of the aesthetic, maybe that of the well-wrought urn: "A story? Something firm, tangible, like a pot with two handles, to be touched and drunk from? . . . A vision, perhaps, if you understand what I mean."[30] These prefatory lines to Wolf's story "June Afternoon" contrast a visionary apprehension of the subject matter to an aesthetic that emphasizes the concreteness of the letter and ways of giving form to it. The tension between these viewpoints provides much of the impetus for Wolf's mode of writing: "I feel keenly the tension between the artistic forms within which we have agreed to abide and the living material, borne to me by my senses, my psychic apparatus, and my thought, which has resisted these forms."[31] It is a little startling to hear Wolf state that she attains knowledge of the living material not only through her senses and her thought but through her "psychic apparatus." Of course, a vision—if I understand what she means—will normally be attained in such a way. Such vision is in fact more normal than we would think, and is not the exclusive province of mystics. It can be as quotidian an affair as hypnagogia, or reading, or writing.

As a writer, Wolf is supposed to work in words rather than in images. But like so many writers, she is deeply ambivalent about words. She criticizes "the centering around Logos, the word as fetish—perhaps the deepest superstition of the West, or at least the one of which I am a fervent devotee" (*Cassandra*, 162). The ironically religious ring of this devotion connects to an observation made shortly before: "The faith in prophets . . . is, to a large extent, faith in the power of the word" (162). Here Wolf's musings on her vocation echo Cassandra's on hers, in the finished novel: "I have always been caught by images more than by words. Probably that is strange, and incompatible with my vocation; but I can no longer pursue my vocation. The last thing in my life will be a picture, not a word. Words die before pictures" (21). In Cassandra's world, prophecy is indeed a matter of the word. Though today we are accustomed to think of the prophet as a seer, all that Cassandra sees in her visionary trances is disbelieved; its source in seeing is too unorthodox, even heretical. This heresy is Wolf's as well. Her writing and Cassandra's seeing are paralleled: Wolf speaks of "the inevitable moment when the woman who writes (who 'sees' in Cassandra's case) no longer represents anything or anyone except herself; but who is that?" (232) One way of answering the question of who you are is through an other. For Wolf, Cassandra is that other, a necessary double: "The longing to produce a double, to express oneself, to pack various lives into this one, to be able to be in several places at once is, I believe, one of the most powerful and least regarded impulses behind writing."[32]

Both Christa Wolf and Cassandra, then, are seers; and both inhabit a world that is eyeless. In a museum on the acropolis, Wolf sees the *korai*, the stone maidens that once supported the porch of the Erechtheum. Eaten away by pollution and acid rain, they have been belatedly removed; they seem to weep blindly. Wolf is deeply moved by the progressive degeneration of these female figures, once fertility goddesses, then architectural supports, now less than that, eloquent in their ruin. Viewing them, Wolf becomes possessed by vision, a vision that is not her own: "A force has come over me. Have the sightless eyes of the *korai* opened up to me? Now I roved through the city with these ancient burning eyes, and I saw today's people, my contemporaries, as descendants" (159). The theme of a novel, she understands, is beginning to make itself known to her, and it is a theme that comprehends the present world as well as the ancient one. The finished novel is framed by statuary that is eyeless, indeed headless. At the book's opening, we are at the gates of Mycenae: "It was here. This is where she stood. These stone lions looked at her; now they no longer have heads." And at the end: "Here is the place. These stone lions looked at her. They seem to move in the shifting light" (3, 138). In the novel that lies between these sentences, Wolf's purpose is to give eyes to the eyeless, to restore the gaze that once saw the living woman, and then to see as she saw. But what is seen by the reader who lends life to Cassandra is a world where seeing is undervalued, overlaid with words. Cassandra realizes that out of words most of all, but also out of silence and ceremony, a second Troy has arisen, "a ghostly city, where we were supposed to feel at home and live at ease" (85). The novel chronicles the gradual derealization of Troy through these elements, which finally permeate even the most intimate recesses of the self: "Isn't the word the very thing that has taken over control of our inner life?"[33]

Against this progressive verbalization, Cassandra opposes her gift of vision. She has received this gift, significantly, in a dream. It is a terrifying dream, in which Apollo appears to her bathed in radiant light, conferring upon her powers of prophecy before demanding her sexual favors in return; when she resists, he transforms himself into a wolf surrounded by mice and spits into her mouth. His gift is no less two-faced; for Cassandra will see the truth, but when she tries to speak it nobody will believe her. In a city built of words, she alone knows how to see. Having received her gift, or curse, in a dream, she continues to rely on her dreams and is criticized by the chief priest for this. Not that the ancient world did not generally rely on dreams. During her trip to Greece, Wolf visits the remains of an *amphiareion*—a center for dream interpretation (stone couches in the open air, potions to induce sleep, priests to read the dreams). But this is not the case in Troy.

In Troy, the closest equivalent to an amphiareion may be the caves above the city to which the women, and a few men, have withdrawn. The caves are carved with images of women: one a goddess, others bringing offerings to her. None of those living in the caves can tell the significance of these images. "Cybele," one woman calls the goddess. Another woman, Arisbe, smiles; she accepts this need to name the images: "Perhaps gradually, without even noticing it, they might come to take the names as a likeness" (124). This, of course, is similar to the process that has built a second, ghostly Troy out of words, displacing the Troy that is seen. Cassandra then asks, "But what do the images stand for?" "That's the question," Arisbe replies. "They stand for the things in us that we do not dare to recognize, that is how it seems to me" (124). These words might suffice for a description of Freudian dream analysis; and it may be significant that after this description Cassandra—who has been brought to the caves broken, well-nigh catatonic—begins to dream again. Her ability to see inside herself the images that others do not dare to recognize contrasts with the need of her people to situate the images of the gods outside. Cassandra asks, "You think that man cannot see himself, Arisbe?" The reply is "That's right. He needs the alien image" (124). And the images of the gods, already alienated from us, may be alienated further by naming them, transforming images into words, their new "likeness."

But at this moment of the novel, of course, words are exactly what we are reading. As Wolf has admitted, art too is a site for "the sinister effects of alienation." Yet these effects can be fought against, here as elsewhere. Framed by the eyeless lions, Wolf's novel is an act of imaging, the words aiming not to replace an image but to bring one before our eyes—if never completely, at least more satisfactorily than through the coarse netting of Aeschylus's lines. Vision, never completely fulfilled, is repeatedly gestured toward, one vision embedded within the other. The first vision is that of the novelist who, following the incentive provided by the present-day image of the fortress of Mycenae, is taken inside it. "Keeping step with the story, I make my way into death." The "I" in the next sentence ("Here I end my days.") is already Cassandra, making her way into the death that awaits her inside the gate. But not yet. The events of her life are envisioned by her as she sits in the chariot while Agamemnon is being murdered inside; she is waiting for her turn. In a state that is both focused and disengaged, she seeks what she barely apprehends: "An image from long, long ago that is floating and that perhaps I can capture if I let my attention wander quietly where it will" (34). And with this image come others, like the shades of the dead in the underworld crowding around the scent of blood. The dead live again in her mind. At the deepest level of her envisioned life are the dreams she has had, visions of yet another kind that drive her through her life and determine the significance of her death. The structure here is like that described by Wolf in one of her essays: "The dreaming woman dreams about the dream another dreamer is having. . . . The spiral keeps turning."[34] And, in a final turn of the spiral, we must not omit our activity as readers, an activity that partakes in the visionary nature of what we are reading about.

Cassandra reminds its readers of their own visionary power: in art, in politics, in the daily business of life. It attempts to bring one woman's vision—Cassandra's or Wolf's—through the net of words so that it may act upon us with all the fascination inherent in the image. Rightly used, words are capable of this: we recall that Apollo, who gave Cassandra her power, is "the god of the seers" as well as the god of poetry. Seeing past this alien god, we can sense his power in ourselves, whether we are writers or readers. It is not really such an unfamiliar power, though it is drawn from unfathomable sources. We sense it in dreams; we sense it in literature. In both of these, the unconscious Other can only play at the elusive threshold of our awareness. Where the unconscious is concerned, we cannot see much. What we can see is that visuality is one of its structuring principles; that its images are intermixed with the language that also structures it; and that interpretive activity, whether the reader's or the author's, is ultimately an interpretation of that which made our selves.

3

Seeing the Forest for the Trees

The fantasmatic self held out as a promise by Lacan's mirror stage is soon translated into the terms of the symbolic. Yet that image is not entirely overwritten by words: "The imagistic and fantasmatic subject of identifications continues, nonetheless, to coexist (in a double inscription) with the subject of language and cultural codes throughout life."[1] Ellie Ragland-Sullivan's reference here to a "double inscription" chimes with what the psychologist Allan Paivio calls the "dual coding theory" of cognition. According to this theory, "the receptive mental work of a reader of literature or a viewer of visual art and the productive work of a creative writer, artist, or scientist involves a continual interplay of two great symbolic systems, one expressed as imagery and the other as language."[2] These two symbolic systems are, roughly, situated in different hemispheres of the brain—left hemisphere for verbal, right hemisphere for imagistic. Each system is capable of accomplishing its mental work without recourse to the other. At the same time that the systems can function independently, they are also interconnected: they may function in tandem for greater effectiveness, switching from verbal to imagistic codes in order to draw upon the strengths of both systems. A painting like Paolo Uccello's *Hunt in the Forest* (Fig. 1), for instance, will naturally be "read" first by the image system. But if the gallery goers linger before Uccello's painting the impressions generated by the images will begin to translate themselves into verbal form. The watchers, that is, will become talkers, speaking perhaps

FIGURE 1. Paolo Uccello, *Hunt in the Forest* (detail). Reproduced by permission of the Ashmolean Museum, Oxford.

about the restless disjunctive movement of the riders in the trees, the geometric look of the tree trunks, the overall sense of a kaleidoscope or hall of mirrors. These last phrases—so clearly pictures, but not the picture on the gallery wall—indicate shifts in the viewer's response, from the verbal system to the imagistic system and back again to the expression of these new images in words. Such a shuttling between systems is characteristic of the richest sort of creative activity by artists, or by those responding to an artist's work.

In this chapter I will examine the ways in which readers shuttle between verbal and visual systems, and the processes by which a visual system is constructed out of a verbal one. I will begin with an image—an image for the verbal code itself and the way that it works. "Woods are a metaphor for the narrative text," Umberto Eco asserted at the outset of his Charles Eliot Norton lectures at Harvard.[3] They "are" this metaphor not just because Eco decrees them to be so, but because they have been used repeatedly, often heatedly, in debates over the nature of textuality. Let us then begin our own hunt in the forest, and do so first with the help of Eco's countryman Italo Calvino.

On the last page of Italo Calvino's *The Baron in the Trees*, a transformation takes place that allows us to see what has been before our eyes all along. We have been reading the story of an eighteenth-century nobleman who, sent from the table at the age of twelve, climbs a tree and vows never to come down. He keeps his word. He sleeps, dines, hunts, has love affairs, writes and philosophizes, dispenses revolutionary counsel, finally dies—all this in the network of branches that makes up the realm of "Ombrosa." Years later, the great trees have vanished, leaving the baron's brother to reflect both on them and on the story he has told us.

Ombrosa no longer exists. Looking at the empty sky, I ask myself if it ever did really exist. That mesh of leaves and twigs of fork and froth, minute and endless, with the sky glimpsed only in sudden specks and splinters, perhaps it was only there so that my brother could pass through it with his tomtit's tread, was embroidered on nothing, like this thread of ink which I have let run on for page after page, swarming with cancellations, corrections, doodles, blots and gaps, bursting at times into clear big berries, coagulating at others into piles of tiny starry seeds, then twisting away, forking off, surrounding buds of phrases with frameworks of leaves and clouds, then interweaving again, and so running on and on and on until it splutters and bursts into a last senseless cluster of words, ideas, dreams, and so ends.[4]

This passage is a remarkable example of the complex shuttling between visual and verbal. The narrator begins by "looking," but what he is looking at is empty sky, for "Ombrosa no longer exists." Did it ever exist? The question does not just reflect the narrator's incredulity at an overwhelmingly present absence. It is also, for the reader, the question that must always be raised about the ontological status of fiction. If the forest of Ombrosa has never existed in a material sense it has nevertheless achieved an *effect* of existence in the readers' minds; for we have seen it. We have seen it in a narrative mode, translating verbal to visual stimuli. This mode is not that different in its effects from the mode of memory that immediately follows in the passage. Against the empty sky the narrator now sees what he has been looking for: the vanished forest of Ombrosa. In his vision, the sky is nearly shut out by the forest's density. But the words that follow suggest that the whole forest is only a pretext (for what, I will be explaining in a moment), and its endless mesh then dwindles to the intimate compass of a piece of embroidery[5]—an embroidery, moreover, on "nothing." Beginning again from that nothing, another kind of fullness succeeds—not the density of fictional vision, now, but of words. We can no longer see Ombrosa, which was always made of words. Yet the words that stimulated that seeing are themselves seen in a vivid evocation of the written page, "swarming with cancellations, corrections, doodles, blots and gaps." And as we continue to read about seeing the words that generated the seeing of Ombrosa, something peculiar begins to happen. The imaged manuscript itself is seen as visually cognate to a forest—a dense and proliferating forest which once again runs down into nothingness, ending in a "cluster" that combines "words, ideas, dreams" without sorting out the relations between them. Only one relation has been established—writing is like a forest—even if this relation leaves everything else to be clarified.

Or almost everything. For we recall that the forest, or the narrative, was perhaps "only there so that my brother could pass through it"—text as pretext. And here the peculiarities of the brother's mode of existence suddenly fall into place and reveal themselves to be those of the writer. Inhabiting a mesh of words, the writer is poised midway between two realms. The first is an always present emptiness, materially represented by the blank page that he tries to cover over, as a forest covers one from the sky. The second is that to which writing refers without ever contacting it directly: the earth and the humans that live and die upon it. Writing is removed from this real existence, but continually refers to it, clothes it, closes over between it and an ultimate emptiness. The last paragraph of Calvino's novel suggests that a kind of allegory has been at work in the whole. The baron in the trees and the writer who gives him to us are brothers, but also perhaps doubles of each other.

The doubling I am concerned with here, though, is the double coding that has made Calvino's point throughout the passage I have analyzed. Throughout Calvino's book we have seen a forest. Only in the final paragraph are we reminded that all we have really seen is writing. What can we say about the relation between these two types of seeing? In this instance, at least, the relation has been as close as that between the terms of a metaphor—Eco's metaphor. While reading we have been lost in a forest. That forest has been seen through words, words which are often described as trees.

A Cluster of Trees

Since Ferdinand de Saussure, the word has been discussed in terms of the relationship between a signifier and its signified—a relationship that may be diagrammed as follows:

TREE

Jacques Lacan reproduces this "classic, yet faulty illustration" in his essay on "The Agency of the Letter in the Unconscious." He then proceeds to correct the diagram's faults, mentally overwriting its visual component—the presumptive signified—with the signifier. He crosses the bar between these by extending the domain of the signifier, dropping it like a verbal curtain before the visual signified. Though the signifier thus dominates the signified, it does not do this in a monolithic way; what descends on the visual tree is not an iron curtain. Lacan specifies that a signifier is not to be simply equated with one signification: "One has only to listen to poetry, which Saussure was no doubt in the habit of doing, for a polyphony to be heard, for it to become clear that all discourse is aligned along the several staves of a score" (154). The horizontal lines of this polyphonic score are of course meant to be read simultaneously—that is, vertically. It is this vertical reading that is stressed in Lacan's next sentence: "There is in effect no signifying chain that does not have, as if attached to the punctuation of each of its units, a whole articulation of relevant contexts suspended 'vertically,' as it were, from that point" (154). These contexts are a culture's multiple associations with the signifier—in this case the word *tree*. "What this structure of the signifying chain discloses is the possibility I have . . . to use it in order to signify *something quite other* than what it says" (155). This "something quite other" is not a reference to some other *object* occupying a place in the world. Ultimately, as we will see, it is the Otherness of the unconscious. If for Lacan the unconscious is structured as a language, language is now visualized as a forest. Lacan makes of the word *tree* an archly polyphonic poetry:

I have only to plant my tree in a locution; climb the tree, even project on to it the cunning illumination a descriptive context gives to a word; raise it (*arborer*) so as not to let myself be imprisoned in some sort of *communiqué* of the facts, however official, and if I know the truth, make it heard, in spite of all the *between-the-lines* censures by the only signifier my acrobatics through the branches of the trees can constitute. (155–56)

The acrobatics are those of "the subject in the search for the true" (155). In these tree branches, which are also the ramifications of language, the subject must move continually, swinging from one branch to another like some linguistic Tarzan, or more sedately like a baron in the trees. For this subject, there is no solid ground.

At this point Lacan gives a name to the kind of signifier he sees being constituted by these acrobatics: the name is *metonymy*. This is one side of "the effective field constituted by the signifier, so that meaning can emerge there" (156). The other side is *metaphor*. Metaphor and metonymy, of course, correspond structurally to the Freudian condensation and displacement. Together they indicate the nature of that "truth" which the locution can express despite all censures: it is the unconscious. Not surprisingly, then, all the meanings that emerge through the "talking cure" of psychoanalysis do so through connections between words: "The letter . . . produces all the effects of truth in man without involving the spirit at all. It is none other than Freud who had this revelation, and he called his discovery the unconscious" (158–59).

That which is between words forms the basis for Luce Irigaray's challenge to Lacan, one that is couched in the same image of trees. Her starting point is that problematic interface between word and image, the rebus:

The fact that the dream can be interpreted only as a "rebus" should have persuaded the "reader" to turn it in all directions and positions, and not favor one type of inscription that would already prescribe a meaning to it. . . . Why not rather have recalled those "pictures" made for children, pictographs in which the hunter and the hunted, and their dramatic relationships, are to be discovered *between* the branches, *made out* from *between* the trees. From the spaces . . . that organize the scene, blanks that sub-tend the scene's structuration.[6]

This passage from *Speculum of the Other Woman* is rich with suggestion. To begin with, it *demands* a forest for meaning to emerge; the single word is not enough. Indeed, Lacan may have inadvertently admitted as much in stating that each of the units in the signifying chain has "a whole articulation of relevant contexts suspended 'vertically,' as it were, from that point." This vertical suspension is later reversed to become the vertical ascension of the branching tree. But what are these branches? The relevant contexts, in Lacan's account, can only be linguistic ones. The tree which is the word can only branch out, in other words, toward other words—which are also trees. Tree necessarily becomes forest: there is no signification without other signifiers. Whether metonymic or metaphoric, words connect with words.

But this "connection" is not a seamless one. Thick as a forest may be, it has spaces. Even the great forest of Ombrosa, like other forests, is a mesh with glimpses of sky, with spaces to pass through, a sense of space behind it reminding us that all these twigs and branches may be "embroidered on nothing." Yet, as in *King Lear*, something can come of this nothing. Irigaray's suggestion is that meaning arises from the spaces *between*. She is thus evading the "materiality" of the letter which Lacan so strongly insists upon in his seminar on "The Purloined Letter." She is also evading the predetermined inscription of meaning by linguistic structures. It is not these structures that organize the scene, all too predictably. Rather the scene is organized by the unpredictable results of juxtaposed words—results that are seen not in the words themselves, but in the spaces between them. Words branch out, reach toward other words: the important thing, however, is not the word that is reached toward but the shape that is outlined by this reaching, this juxtaposition. That shape is as unpredictable as the multifarious combinations of innumerable unique words. Though these words may be classified according to linguistic structures, and be governed by them to a degree, such structures will never be adequate to the inexhaustible variety of finer structures (leaf and twig, shifting light and shadow) capable of being produced, and continually being produced. The meaning of these cannot be prescribed or inscribed before the fact: it arises not from linguistic structures but from what they border and outline: "the spaces . . . that organize the scene, blanks that sub-tend the scene's structuration."

Moreover, if the shape of meaning thus produced is unpredictable, it is also unstable: the dream, as much of a pictograph as the child's game, must be turned "in all directions and positions." Likewise, no one position in reading is adequate to all the possibilities of shape and meaning. In the child's game, hunter and hunted emerge only in varying angles; so in the text there is no stable horizon of expectation, no ruled line to orient a meaning that will arise as inevitably as the sun.

Irigaray's use of textual spaces can be compared to that of Roman In-garden. In *The Cognition of the Literary Work of Art*, Ingarden recognizes that there are spaces in the text the reader fills in, but this is merely an un-fortunate distraction: "The reader then reads 'between the lines' and in-voluntarily complements many of the sides of portrayed objectivities not determined in the text itself, through an 'overexplicit' understanding of the sentences and especially of the nouns appearing in them. I call this com-plementing determination the 'concretization' of the portrayed objects."[7] Later, Ingarden opposes the study of literary works of art to these con-cretizations (234). They are "involuntary," "overexplicit," and a positive danger to the critical project. For Ingarden, reading "between the lines" in-terferes with critical objectivity. For Lacan, the truth makes itself heard "in spite of all the *between-the-lines* censures"—the censoring activity through which we try to avoid the words of the signifying chain which is our fate. But for Irigaray, it is precisely between the lines that we find meaning be-ing made, in a continual and ever-changing process.

Irigaray's "meaning" is not made abstractly, like a philosophical prop-osition, but through the senses, in particular through seeing. The text is compared to a pictograph, not unlike a dream or a children's game, thus implying a visual element in the verbal. How may this visual element of the text be perceived? One answer is suggested by a picture, and moreover one which recapitulates Irigaray's "hunter and hunted," though in a differ-ent key. That picture is Magritte's *Le blanc-seing* (Fig. 2). The title is a somewhat archaic term having to do with documents. But while a docu-ment is ordinarily fully written except for the signature blank, the *blanc-seing* reverses this: everything is blank *except* the signature. Placed on a white page, the signature authorizes you to fill in whatever you wish; you determine what is to be read above that signature.[8] Magritte's painting, in keeping with his philosophical and literary concerns, may then allude to a filling-in process like that described by Ingarden.

A loosely spaced forest divides the canvas into vertical strips, of which some are tree trunks and others the spaces between them, filled with distant foliage and sky. Through this forest—or rather through these strips—pass a horse and rider, intersected now by a trunk, now by a space, now by a faraway trunk treated as if it were near. The picture is an optical witticism, a trick on the conventions of paint and perception, flatness and depth. And it is more than this. We cannot resist filling in the blanks to

FIGURE 2. René Magritte, *Le Blanc-seing* (1965). Collection of Mr. and Mrs. Paul Mellon, National Gallery of Art, Washington, D.C. Photograph © Board of Trustees, National Gallery of Art.

create a stable image. Yet this attempt only underscores the shifting perceptual rhythm that characterizes what we see, what emerges from this forest: Wallace Stevens's "noble rider" maybe. For words are implicated here.
Something like this happens in the relation between our verbal and visual
perceptions of the text.

We may approach that relation through Foucault's commentary on
another painting by Magritte, *This Is Not a Pipe*. The legend inscribed in
Magritte's painting sets up a complex tension with the clear depiction of
the pipe above it—a tension between, among other things, the verbal and
the visual. For Foucault this tension is compressed and summed up in the
calligram, that text shaped as picture which refuses to be read as both simultaneously. One can only alternate perceptions, as in the rabbit-duck diagram (another child's game) analyzed by Gombrich and by Wittgenstein.

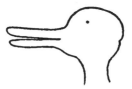

So Foucault sums up: "The calligram never speaks and represents at
the same moment. The very thing that is both seen and read is hushed in
the vision, hidden in the reading."[9] The calligram is a species of pictograph
like those of which Irigaray speaks. But she speaks of the pictograph in order to speak of reading. So we are led to a possibility beyond the one that
Foucault is considering: "The very thing that is both seen and read" may
be reading itself.

This possibility first of all suggests a return to the trees of Lacan and
Irigaray. Lacan's materiality of the letter, Irigaray's spaces—both are partial
metaphors for a whole that is neither and both. The materiality of Lacan's
letter, as Derrida has argued in *The Post Card*, must divide itself, must be
implicated with space, if it is to be transmissible at all. On the other hand,
Irigaray's spaces take on the shapes of what we seek and see only through
their material definitions. Neither writer has the last word on the word,
which exists in both aspects simultaneously, in a kind of figure-ground
relation. "Meaning," according to Paivio's dual coding theory, emerges
through shifts in perception—and this is so whether what we "see" is rela-
tively abstract (and yet, I suspect, never entirely free of a metaphoric-visual

component) or whether it is the fantasm produced by a vividly written work of fiction.

Where Lacan has expelled "spirit" it seems that I have reinstated "perception." In so doing, I touch on Wolfgang Iser's version of reader response, which is in its own way a perceptual one. Criticizing Ingarden, Iser writes: "For him, concretization was just the actualization of the potential element of the work. It was not an interaction between text and reader."[10] Yet Iser curiously limits that interaction. Avoiding Ingarden's mechanistic notions of filling in, he speaks of syntheses below the threshold of consciousness, which he calls "passive syntheses." Of such syntheses the basic element is the image. The nature of our perception of the image is not to be considered, though, except as involved in "theme" and "significance": "The mental image of passive synthesis is something which accompanies our reading—and is not itself the object of our attention, even when these images link up into a whole panorama" (136). But why should it not be the object of our attention, as it is often the object of our reading, a primary aspect of our pleasure in reading?

Hide and Seek

This aspect is currently becoming the conscious subject matter of literature, part of a tendency for contemporary authors to write novels not (as they used to) about writing novels but about reading them. The main characters of these novels are either readers or characters who are *being* read, as in Dennis Potter's *Hide and Seek*.

We enter the first part of *Hide and Seek*, entitled "Into the Forest," through the consciousness of Daniel Miller, a character who knows he is a character in a novel. It is terrifying to him to know that his smallest gesture and thought (including that knowledge and that terror) are in the hands of the Author. To escape him, to hide from him, has become Miller's obsessive purpose. The question is whether there *is* any place to hide. He recalls words from the Sunday mornings of his childhood, words about another Author: "Can any hide himself in secret places that I shall not see him? saith the Lord. Do not I fill heaven and earth?" The Author, when we meet him, has the same childhood recollections and applies the words to himself: "The narrator of a novel can do anything, with the people, the things, the machines, the landscape, the lot. Can any hide in his pages that he shall not see him? Does not he fill in every word from cover to cover?" (163). Miller hopes not: "There must also be meaningful senses in which a character, any character, did not wholly belong to his Author. At the very least there should be some untenanted space between the Author's mind and the Author's hand or between the thought thought and the written thought" (3).

The tension here is like that between Lacan and Irigaray on the nature of words. Is the signifying chain a fatal omnipotence or are there spaces between, through which an undetermined meaning (or possibly even a character) can escape? Those spaces, and/or that which they are filled with from cover to cover, make up fiction; but, in the opening section of Potter's novel, they also make up a forest, fiction *as* forest. Miller has come to the forest to seek a cottage he has rented, sight unseen, in which he hopes to hide. But he is now lost in that ambiguous landscape; a more generous selection will exemplify the shifts of perception characteristic of this novel:

He is tired and confused after almost four hours of hand-hurt at the wheel. The gloom outside seems to be coming from inside his head: and *that* gloom, he thought he knew, could be followed all the way back or all the way forward along the upward slopes and downward loops of words, words, words, words. Words on a page, on several pages, composed out of the malignant and sex-sodden chaos inside the Author's head.

The malformed shapes outside the car windows also appeared to be shifting about inside his head. Daniel knew they were being imposed upon him. He knew that soon these shapes, these uneasily defined lineaments of dusk, would begin to lack all observable configuration as they moved even more uncompromisingly into the ink-soaked pus of his brain.

"I would be grateful," he said, almost out loud, "if you will let me have some more light, you big prick."

Too truculent!

The trees all around nodded secretively together and then, decisively, closed in towards each other, twig feeling for twig, branch meeting branch, trunks bending slowly with thuggish determination. An old trick of the Author, this, intimidating Daniel with hostile jumps of perspective, inexplicable thickenings of light, and swift spurts of sticky sadness. (9)

The fear of thickening, of words closing over the last possible spaces between them, has its counterpart in another and opposite fear. Suffering from swollen joints, Miller imagines himself being pumped up by the Author with bubble after bubble of pain: "If it kept up like this, pump pump, he would fill up like a balloon, swell up until, unanchored, he would float away into the illiterate void above the schematic trees" (19). Pure space, then, has its own terrors, if it is not space *between*.

Lost in the forest, Miller finds himself trapped in recurring words: "But he had seen this before. He had been on that page" (29). In a parody of narrative repetition, handled with great subtlety elsewhere in the novel, the words here run the character on a treadmill; or an endlessly repeating loop of tape or film; or perhaps merely a long circling road whose turnoff is always missed in the darkness. As with the repetition compulsion, though, this apparently futile process may sometimes provide a psychological clue: "He was getting nearer to himself, travelling on a long loop of bumpy path through the trees" (136). Reassuring—but not to Daniel, perhaps. For "he" at this point is the Author, as he returns once more to his manuscript. And yet he is Daniel as well: the loop is in effect a Möbius strip. Author and character are one (it is impossible to get "nearer to himself") and neither can escape to the other side; there *is* no "other side" of the piece of paper which is the page. In the bulk of Potter's book we watch the Author fighting this fact, trying to hide his connection with his character and through that very act establishing it. We watch him rewrite his experiences now in the first person, now in the third, now in the guise of Daniel Miller—a dense interweaving of variations and shifting perspectives repeatedly rendered in the image of a forest, a forest of writing:

The foolscap sheets of Croxley Script ("the all purpose paper") were by now beginning to look like an inventive infant's representation of woodland scenery illicitly sketched on top of pages already thick with words. Individual adjectives and adverbs had been obliterated by a tight foliage of tangled afterthought, single sentences were submerged in blotchily leaved overgrowth, narrow black paths of muddied fear meandered between the rustling syntax, and whole paragraphs were lost beneath the heavy lattice of trunk-thick deletions. He had come now in the mid-passage of his life to a forest dark and he had lost the straight path. The words were leading him the wrong way. (135)

Philosophical Fiction

Lost in the woods of narrative, then, what do we find? In a perceptual hide and seek we lose the word to find the image, lose the image in the word. Reading, it seems, proceeds in rhythms, risings and fallings and alterations of perception which are not the least compelling element of the experience of being "lost in a book." But can we detect any configuration of pleasure or knowledge underlying these shifting perceptions?

One answer is implied, ironically enough, in the course of an attack on the very notion of readerly visualization. The attack is spread out over the first four essays in William Gass's *Fiction and the Figures of Life*, but it can be summed up in this passage from "Philosophy and the Form of Fiction":

Strictly speaking style cannot be, itself, a kind of vision, the notion is very misleading, for we do not have before us some real forest which we might feel ourselves free to render in any number of different ways; we have only the words which make up this one. There are no descriptions in fiction, there are only constructions, and the principles which govern these constructions are persistently philosophical.[11]

In "The Concept of Character in Fiction," Gass makes his case using a character from Henry James's *The Awkward Age*. Here are James's words: "Mr. Cashmore, who would have been very red-headed if he had not been very bald, showed a single eyeglass and a long upper lip; he was large and jaunty, with little petulant movements and intense ejaculations that were not in the line of his type." We do not *see* Mr. Cashmore as we see objects in the real world, Gass points out. There are too many things omitted: the nose, the eyes behind the eyeglass, the neck and chin and ears, to list only a few; and the single word "large" gives us no idea of how the character's weight is distributed or how much there is to distribute. There is also the contradictory matter of his redheadedness, which is not apparent because his baldness is; and finally, Mr. Cashmore is typified by certain actions that are "not in the line of his type." "Mr. Cashmore has what he's been given," Gass concludes; "he also *has* what he *hasn't*, just as strongly" (45). But with this "just as strongly" Gass opens up both the text and his own argument. For he is here giving equal force to what is seen and what is not seen (in Mr. Cashmore's redheadedness and his "type" James is doing much the same thing). And what is "not seen" need not only be equated with words, as in Foucault's rather binary perceptual model. Rather, the "not seen" here turns back to Irigaray's blanks—blanks which may be filled with visualizations but in relation to the verbal may also be apprehended *as* blanks: one thinks of the strips of "space" between the trees, foregrounded in Magritte's

Le Blanc-seing. Repeatedly we have encountered a shifting, combinatory play between foreground and background, visual and verbal, blank and filled. All this suggests that the reading experience is, beyond specific content, structured as a play with perception—an intelligent play, indeed a philosophical play.

Gass sees as "persistently philosophical" the principles governing fictional constructions: "As a set of sensations Mr. Cashmore is simply impossible; as an idea he is admirably pungent and precise" (46). But is he? I am not at all sure that Mr. Cashmore is a philosophical idea, let alone a precise one. But for the sake of argument let us say he is. We may then ask whether Mr. Cashmore's ontological status becomes any clearer. What is the ontological status of a philosophical idea? Is it clearer than a visual idea? Is it altogether free of the visual idea? Is it a reality in the world in the same way that a tree is? Or is it an "unreality" akin to that of fictional objects? Is it, in fact, a fiction? Gass seems to think so.

"So much of philosophy is fiction," begins the essay "Philosophy and the Form of Fiction." "Novelist and philosopher are both obsessed with language," Gass continues, "and make themselves up out of concepts. Both, in a way, create worlds." Yet, Gass argues, the philosopher's more encompassing fiction is supreme. "Philosophers multiply our general nouns and verbs; they give fresh sense to stale terms; 'man' and 'nature' are their characters; while novelists toil at filling in the blanks in proper names and at creating other singular affairs" (4). The basic contrast here is between the novelist's "singular" and the philosopher's "general." However, I am not going to let pass that reference to "filling in the blanks." Clearly novelists do not fill in the blanks; certainly James has not done so in the case of Mr. Cashmore. Novelists could never fill in all the blanks if they wanted to—but they do not want to. First of all, they don't need to; the novel, according to Gass himself, "can succeed only through the cooperating imagination and intelligence of its consumers, who fill out, for themselves, the artist's world and make it round." (23). Yet this filling out on one's own terms, Gass asserts in "The Concept of Character in Fiction," may often interfere with the terms of the work.

The ultimate terms of the work, though, depend on what is *not* filled in. The shifting status of the blank in relationship to word and image; the sense of something always to be filled in, but also the sense of what cannot ever be filled in; the oscillation between what is seen and what is not seen, what is understood and not understood; the constant sense of trajectory over the text's spaces—these are the conditions of reading, and of the reader. They are the conditions on which we read the world in which we find ourselves, whether it is fictional or real. In its continual *process* the act of reading reminds us, within the borders of play, of our paradigmatic ways of making sense of the world. These ways matter more than any particular sense that is made. This is how I would explicate an observation that Gass throws out in passing: "Fiction, in the manner of its making, is pure philosophy" (3).

Constructing Vision

Fiction, "in the manner of its making," reflects the ways that we see the world—and does so quite literally. To demonstrate this I will turn to David Marr's influential book *Vision*, where vision is analyzed as information processing. The process of apprehending shape, for instance, proceeds on a continuum ranging from a two-dimensional "primal sketch" through a "2½-D sketch"—which establishes the depth and orientation of certain key points relative to the viewer—to full visual realization of the perceived object in three dimensions. And all of these modeling modes are employed by us in rapid succession to organize and interpret light's retinal stimulation. The commonsense objection to this sequenced series of models is of course that one's perceptual experience seems much more complete than this. Marr responds to this objection in a no less commonsense way (he has appended "A Conversation" to *Vision* in order to express the important aspects of his theory in less technical language than that employed in the body of his book):

Well, first remember that our visual processes can work extremely rapidly. The time between requesting information about a part of the visual field and moving the eyes there, getting it, and linking it to a 3-D model is probably usually under half a second. The second thing is, How much of a novel scene can you recall if you look at it only very briefly? Not very much! Its coarse organization, or perhaps one or two details. And once you close your eyes, the richness is gone, isn't it? I think that the richness corresponds to what is available now, at the pure perceptual level, and what you can remember immediately is much more closely related to the 3-D model description that you create for it while your eyes are open.[12]

Let's first consider the "coarse organization" which remains after only a brief glimpse, and which for Marr corresponds to a modeling process in vision. Elsewhere in "A Conversation" he explains by reference to certain parallel effects in language the way that this coarse organization comes about. He is arguing that any object or action can actually give rise simultaneously to several different "coarse" internal descriptions. Out of these an appropriate overall scenario is chosen. This, he says, is like what happens in verbal scenarios:

If one reads
>   The fly buzzed irritatingly on the windowpane.
>   John picked up a newspaper.
the immediate inference is that John's intentions toward the fly are fundamentally malicious. If he had picked up the telephone, the inference would be less secure. It is generally agreed that an "insect-damaging scenario" is somehow deployed during the reading of these sentences. (368)

The scenario here arises not out of either sentence but from the configuration of their conjunction—the space between, to adopt Irigaray's terms. There is no reason, then, that a visual scenario should not equally well arise from this sort of conjunction. It may, for instance, arise from the spaces between the words used to construct Mr. Cashmore—especially when some of those words ostentatiously function *as* spaces.

The visual scenario that emerges will not, of course, have the vividness of actual perception. It will correspond much more to the "coarse organization" with "one or two details" which is characteristic of Marr's visual models. John Ashbery describes a similar model of seeing in his poem "Tapestry":

>   The eyesight, seen as inner,
>   Registers over the impact of itself
>   Receiving phenomena, and in so doing
>   Draws an outline, or a blueprint,
>   Of what was just there.[13]

Marr's models can be "seen" only in the absence of direct perceptual stimulation, of "what was just there." In effect what Marr is saying is "To see how we see, close your eyes." This closed-eye seeing is related to the way we see in reading, cast wholly into an eyesight that is "inner." It is also related to memory images, which are similarly removed from what was there:

Marr compares his models to what you can "recall" after a brief glimpse, "remember" with your eyes closed. So the psychologist Stephen Kosslyn has taken an approach to memory images that is parallel to that taken by David Marr for perceptual images.[14] Like Marr, he uses a computational model; he has indeed used actual computer simulations to verify his theories. For Kosslyn, memory images are the end products of constructive processes. These processes are a series of increasingly elaborate models, which generate a picture in much the same way that a picture is generated on the computer screen through a complex series of instructions.

Whether the image produced is mental or perceptual, then, the mind's role is a constructive one: the image is assembled through a series of modeling acts of increasing complexity. This series may not run its full course, in the case of mental visualization: from the outset, scientific investigators found wide discrepancies between people's abilities to visualize mentally.[15] And, of course, the series of modeling acts that makes up mental visualization will not be completed to the same degree as in actual physical seeing—if it is, we have to do with hallucination, disturbing precisely because its images have the force of physical perception. For most mental imagers, the image will obviously be less vivid than in life, less fully realized. But in what ways? What mode of seeing will the mental images take? That is, aside from the nature of the specific object seen, what is the nature of that seeing? Will it be, for instance, schematic? Blurred? Colored (or not)? Intensely focused at points but fading at the periphery? The answers to such questions have not been sought at great length by psychologists, and perhaps for good reasons. To visualize the mode of visualizing, and then to verbalize it, is a very difficult job for experimental subjects who may not have the introspective discrimination required; and the responses of subjects are bound to vary widely with their capacities for visualization. We can get some idea of the look of internal imagery, though, by reading the reports of writers. And here again Calvino serves us well.

The second chapter of Calvino's *If on a Winter's Night a Traveller* is the first chapter of a novel that "you" are described as reading, a novel called *If on a Winter's Night a Traveller*:

The novel begins in a railway station, a locomotive huffs, steam from a piston covers the opening of the chapter, a cloud of smoke hides part of the first paragraph. In the odor of the station there is a passing whiff of station café odor. There is someone looking through the befogged glass, he opens the glass door of the bar, everything is misty, inside, too, as if seen by nearsighted eyes, or eyes irritated by coal dust. The pages of the book are clouded like the windows of an old train, the cloud of smoke rests on the sentences. It is a rainy evening; the man enters the bar; he unbuttons his damp overcoat; a cloud of steam enfolds him; a whistle dies away along tracks that are glistening with rain, as far as the eye can see.[16]

This description mimics the process of settling into a novel's world, which is almost never an immediate or easy transition from the material world. As a novel begins, consequently, we are likely to be more aware of what is involved in the processes of reading. The first sentence makes explicit a shifting between the verbal nature of the physical page and certain visual effects. Those visual effects, however, are reluctant to come into fully focused realization. The text does not provide a clear window into the fictional world but a vaguely translucent one: "The pages of the book are clouded like the windows of an old train." But because these particular pages are our entry point into the novel's visualized world, they are also literalized as the "befogged glass" of the café door. As the reader enters, "everything is misty, inside, too, as if seen by nearsighted eyes, or eyes irritated by coal dust." Prevalent in this description of reading are steam, smoke, fog, mist, and myopia. These are common metaphors for the properties of visual imaging, according to Elaine Scarry:

Some physical objects have features that more closely approximate the phenomenology of imaginary objects than do others. In fact so true is this that we often speak of actual mist, actual gauze, filmy curtains, fog, and blurry rain as dreamlike. Gibson, in fact, explicitly notices that the four key ways in which light ordinarily exposes the structure of the material world—slant, reflectance, intrinsic color, illumination—are absent or "indeterminate" in fog; and thus we may say that in fog the physical universe approaches the condition of the imagination.[17]

This "condition of the imagination" is, as I have noted, not the same for everybody; nor need it remain the same for any one reader. As the novel's dimly apprehended scene is filled in, part by part, by the words on the page, details begin to hang together to create a coherent space—which for Scarry is crucial: "It is impossible to create imaginary persons if one has not created a space for them" (7). Rather like Marr's "2½-D sketch," the spatial relationships of the scene are established through described "patches," which establish points for orienting us in a space enclosed by solidity.

That space, of course, can never be fully filled in by the explicit words of the text. The filling-in takes place in the readerly imagination through memory, in two ways. First, it takes place by holding in memory the details of a fictional room, let us say, that necessarily can come into being only one detail at a time. The more details that are given, the more fully visualized the room becomes. Still, it will always have an amorphous quality: "The lights of the station and the sentences you are reading seem to have the job of dissolving more than of indicating the things that surface from a veil of darkness and fog," writes Calvino.[18] Thus the room is always ready to shift its walls or its decor if a detail is introduced that does not conform to the picture the reader has been building up so far. Calvino notes that several pages into *If on a Winter's Night a Traveller* it is still not clear whether this is a station café of the past or of the present; the reader must be ready to revise certain details of the scene accordingly.

The station café is built up not only through the particular words that are presented for visualization, but also by some sense of what lies between those visualized points. And here the reader draws upon memory in a second way, using appropriate memory images already possessed in order to fill in the blanks. As Calvino says, "Stations are all alike; it doesn't matter if the lights cannot illuminate beyond their blurred halo, all of this is a setting you know by heart" (11). As this filling-in process continues, using both the memory elicited by the text and the memory of stations already experienced outside of the text, it gradually produces the effect of "vivacity," as Scarry has called it. So the foggy quality of the images in Calvino's opening is clarified by the end of the paragraph as the entry into the book is completed: "A whistle dies away along tracks that are glistening with rain, as far as the eye can see." Significantly, the seeing here is precisely not that presented to the eye of the person who has entered the bar and is unbuttoning his overcoat; it seems rather to be a subtle comment on the process of reading, the explicit subject of Calvino's novel and of this passage. What "dies away" with the whistle is the indistinct quality that has characterized visualization throughout the passage. The "blurry rain" that is one of Scarry's listed equivalents of imagination is over, and only its aftermath is described: tracks "glistening with rain, as far as the eye can see." The last phrase indicates an eye that is no longer muffled, myopic, blurred, but one focused on a clearly delineated space. We are "inside" the book's space now, and the process of constructing a modeled image has been played through in all its stages—though it always remains to be done again, with increasing scope and elaboration, as the novel progresses.

The problem of the mode of a reader's imagery is approached in quite a different way by Gilbert Sorrentino in his novel *Mulligan Stew*. While Calvino's implied speculations on the ways that we visualize are presented through a reader, Sorrentino's point of view is that of a character in a novel. In this case the novel is a bad one. The character, Martin Halpin, resents being constantly on call for an inferior writer who has stuck him in a log cabin with a dead body and no clear idea of what he is supposed to do next. While waiting for the novelist's infrequent bouts of inspiration, Halpin and the body exchange gripes and reminisce about other, better gigs they have had. Eventually they come up with a bright idea: since the body never says or does anything, and is unlikely to do so unless there is a sudden flashback, there is no reason for both of them to stay in the cabin. The characters have never been properly described, so either of them can be Halpin if the circumstances demand it, thus freeing the other to get out of the cabin for a breath of fresh air. Here is Halpin's description of his first excursion:

I left the cabin and began walking down the road that runs roughly parallel to the lake. It was straight and totally anonymous, and the trees along it, for all I know of them, were all the same as far as I could tell—same shape, height, color, etc. They were trees in a kind of generic way, "typical" trees. They looked amazingly like drawings. . . . After about a quarter of a mile, I turned and looked back toward the cabin. There it sat, certainly recognizable, but curiously odd-angled, strangely lopsided in effect, as if lacking first one dimension, then another. At one point, as I shifted position, the cabin actually seemed to have no depth at all. Even more curious (I might even say chilling) was that the upper story, viewed now from the *outside*, was no more substantial than the same story *inside*. The house simply fades away into a vague indeterminate blueness that I suddenly realized was the sky. It was as if the upper story of the house was there, but made of a seamless glass, so that one could "sense" it, but not actually see it. I turned away and continued down the road, past hundreds more of the disheartening trees.[19]

As Halpin observes, the curious properties of the cabin here correspond to its properties from the inside, described in an earlier chapter: "At the side of the living room, a staircase leads 'nowhere.' Oh, I don't mean to say that it disappears into empty space, it simply leads to a kind of . . . haziness, in which one knows there is *supposed* to be a hallway and bedroom doors: but there is absolutely nothing" (30). What Sorrentino has done here, through Halpin, is to literalize certain common properties of literary visualization.

The "haziness" corresponds to the imaginative indistinctness out of which, if the author set himself to it, a more fully realized environment might emerge. The trees have managed to realize themselves, but only in a schematic way. Still, according to both Marr and Kosslyn, this schematic stage is a component in both physical vision and mental imaging. The author's ineptness has carried through the process only part of the way. Sorrentino uses this inept author, as Calvino uses his reader, to make us more aware of the sequence and nature of that visualizing process.

The Ground of the Self's Figure

I have said that the unrealized world of the novel is filled in not only through an accumulation of verbal cues, but also through recourse to the reader's own memories. If this is so, there is not only shifting between verbal and visual systems; a certain shifting also takes place between what could be described as foreground and background. It has been so described by Wolfgang Iser:

> In reading there are these two levels—the alien "me" and the real, virtual "me"—which are never cut off from each other. Indeed, we can only make someone else's thoughts into an absorbing theme for ourselves, provided the virtual background of our own personality can adapt to it. Every text we read draws a different boundary within our personality, so that the virtual background (the real "me") will take on a different form, according to the theme of the text concerned. This is inevitable, if only for the fact that the relationship between alien theme and virtual background is what makes it possible for the unfamiliar to be understood.[20]

Iser here approaches the paradoxical language of figure and ground. The real "me" (and actually, "real" should be in quotation marks as well) is described as background for the reading experience. But during that experience it will "take on a different form." The fact that it takes on form at all makes it now a figure. The logical extension would seem to be that the alien "me" would become ground for that figure. And in a sense it does do that: it has provided the ground on which the self has called forth its stock of memories to be disposed in a new configuration. Moreover, because that figure is made up of mental images from the reader's own memory, and because the construction of this figure has been a product of the reader's own activity, the *alienness* of what Iser calls "the alien 'me'" recedes. We are then said to "identify" with a character who is other than ourselves—who is nevertheless to a great degree made up of and by ourselves. Our "selves," in more versions than one, thus oscillate continually during the act of reading.

That our self is unstable, an assemblage of potential identities in process, is not an insight peculiar to postmodernism. Virginia Woolf, that icon of modernity, makes a similar point in *To the Lighthouse*, through the musings of Mrs. Ramsay on the pleasures of losing "personality":

This self having shed its attachments was free for the strangest adventures. When life sank down for a moment, the range of experience seemed limitless. . . . Beneath it is all dark, it is all spreading, it is unfathomably deep; but now and again we rise to the surface and that is what you see us by. Her horizon seemed to her limitless. There were all the places she had not seen; the Indian plains; she felt herself pushing aside the thick leather curtain of a church in Rome.[21]

With this last vivid detail, Mrs. Ramsay is no longer verbalizing to herself the pleasures of losing personality; she is experiencing them, losing one personality and finding herself embodied in another one—if only for an imaginative instant. That instant is enough to indicate the potential for more extended experiences—a potential that is activated during the process of "identifying" with what we read. In reading, according to Iser, "we have the apparently paradoxical situation in which the reader is forced to reveal aspects of himself in order to experience a reality that is different from his own" (132–33).

There is in fact a scene of reading in *To the Lighthouse*, which concludes the first part of the novel. Husband and wife are alone together in the sitting room, each lost in a book. We will look into Mrs. Ramsay's book, and into her mind:

She opened the book and began reading here and there at random, and as she did so she felt that she was climbing backwards, upwards, shoving her way up under petals that curved over her, so that she only knew this is white, or this is red. She did not know at first what the words meant at all.

Steer, hither steer your winged pines, all beaten Mariners

she read and turned the page, swinging herself, zig-zagging this way and that, from one line to another as from one branch to another. (137)

Here no identification takes place (the fact that Mrs. Ramsay is reading poetry rather than fiction accounts for this in part); indeed what takes place does so even though "she did not know at first what the words meant at all."

Yet words may have effects apart from their meanings. For some readers they may have a synesthetic effect, as the next chapter will explain; consequently, white and red petals. Some readers will be affected by what has been called "syntactic imagery," where the shape and rhythm of sentences can express a nonverbal perception;[22] so there is the sense of a particular movement in space in relation to branches and oversized flowers. That movement is like Lacan's description of how the subject moves through the poetic ramifications of the signifying trees. The subject performs its "acrobatics through the branches of the trees" in search of the true—which is for Lacan the unconscious. The unconscious may also be what Mrs. Ramsay is seeking, and has described earlier as a spreading darkness beneath—"Now and again we rise to the surface and that is what you see us by." But at the end of her long day Mrs. Ramsay does not want to rise to the surface or to be seen—not even in another guise, another possible self that desires and strives. For, as she has said earlier, "losing personality, one lost the fret, the hurry, the stir" (73). Admittedly, Mrs. Ramsay conceives of the unconscious as being a good deal more stable than does Lacan. For Lacan, there is no resting place for the subject moving through the forest of language, and unable ever to emerge from it—which gives a twist certainly not intended by Woolf to the lines that Mrs. Ramsay murmurs as she is reaching for her book:

> And all the lives we ever lived,
> And all the lives to be,
> Are full of trees and changing leaves.

Despite their differences, though, these two readers of poetry both move through the branching words in a parallel search for that which is other than "self."

If what they are searching for is the unconscious, in a sense they already have it. They have it not merely in its commonly conceived form, lying hidden inside, beneath, like a darkness wherein secrets may be found; for the most ordinary daylight processes are largely unconscious. Seeing, remembering, reading—the images that arise in each case are constituted out of absences as much as presences, and in ways of which we cannot be fully conscious. To be conscious of one's "self," then, to be self-conscious, is always a problematic and paradoxical activity. For the philosopher Ernst Bloch it is one that can be summed up and imaged as a walk in the forest:

> We walk in the forest and feel we are or might be what the forest is dreaming. We pass between the pillars of its tree-trunks, small, spiritual, and invisible to ourselves, as their sound, as that which could not become forest again or external appearance of day and visibility. We do not possess it, that which all this around us—moss, curious flowers, roots, trunks and streaks of light—is or signifies, because we are it itself and are standing too close to it, the spectral and still ineffable nature of consciousness or interiorisation.[23]

A dense forest indeed. This passage, from the beginning of Bloch's long essay "The Philosophy of Music," is resonant with paradoxes and disconcerting shifts. The shifts, we will see, constitute its subject—in a punning sense, since Bloch here is meditating on how the subject may be figured, and finds for it no stable ground.

The walk in the forest raises the question of what "we are" in contrast to the material objects around us. For to ourselves we seem to be different from the visible physical world. We are "spiritual" and "invisible to ourselves"; we cannot become, to ourselves, "external appearance of day and visibility." At the same time we are necessarily in some relation to the objects around us, to these trees. We are "their sound"—perhaps we are the answer to the old puzzler "If a tree falls in the forest when nobody is there to hear it, is there a sound?" We are also, perhaps, "what the forest is dreaming"; invisible as we are, we feel ourselves to be the unconscious of the consciously apprehended world. This may seem like aggrandizement, implying as it does that we are the focus of the natural world. However, a slight shift allows us to see this process as diminution (we are "small"), since we are the dreamed, not the dreamer; Carroll's Alice, lost in another wood, knew how disturbing this possibility could be. In a sense we are constituted *by* the forest's sound—as well as all its sights, smells, movements. "Moss, curious flowers, roots, trunks and streaks of light"—all that is around us we are, in the act of perceiving it: "We are it itself." We do not possess the forest because that implies a separateness from it; it would be more accurate to say we are possessed by it.

What Bloch means by saying that we are "standing too close to it" is probably connected to his theories about the immediate present, the "now." The nature of the now, Bloch argues in *The Principle of Hope*, is to be hollow, to be a blank. This he illustrates by a visual phenomenon common in landscape painting where the foreground—that is, that part of the landscape to which its perceivers stand closest—is ill defined or even undefined; definition and composition come into being with distance. In time, too, significance is never inherent in the moment of the now, which Bloch describes as a "fermenting Not."[24] He distinguishes this Not from Nothing: "The Not is of course emptiness, but at the same time the drive to break out of it; in hunger, in privation, the emptiness mediates itself precisely as horror vacui, precisely therefore as *abhorrence of the Not at the Nothing*" (306). The Not, which seems to be a species of lack, extends itself to the Not-yet, to an anticipation of realization. And this realization, continually deferred, continually anticipated, moves us into the future. It does so without our ever comprehending fully the present, where perceptual lack is as much of an element as the overwhelming fullness of the physical world around us. Thus, in the concluding sentence of Bloch's walk in the forest, consciousness—here equated with interiorization of the external world—is "spectral and still ineffable." Much of the nature of consciousness, that is, must be inaccessible to its subjects; the line between the conscious and the unconscious blurs.

This philosophical speculation on the shifts between conscious and unconscious, subject and object, foreground and background is pertinent to reading, which enacts similar processes. For reading too has its now, a blank or *blanc-seing* to be filled in by the reader. The source of that filling-in must be the reader's multifarious self, but not only that self. Passing through the woods of narrative, self is continually intersected by words—words that function now as foreground, now as background to the equally unstable figurations of fictional identity. And ours. "Whatever we shape leads back around ourselves again," Bloch asserts just before the passage I have cited. The shaping processes of fiction, then, say something about the ways we shape our perceptions of the world, and of our selves. In this sense, Gass's statement is vindicated: "Fiction, in the manner of its making, is pure philosophy." This "pure" philosophy, however, is not abstract but experiential. In reading fiction we do not see a concept, though concepts may load the rifts with ore. Rather, fiction causes us to see "moss, curious flowers, roots, trunks and streaks of light"—the richness of the perceptual world, and something of our ways of perceiving it. For no matter how vivid our apprehension, it is removed by some degrees from direct perception. This removal, as David Marr has suggested, may help to foreground the dynamics by which we model our perceptions to ourselves. Whatever else we may see on the printed page, we are constantly seeing words and images change places with one another. The visualization of fiction—fleeting and vague though it may be—therefore has a purpose beyond what is commonly allowed by its critics. It is more than a distraction, an escape, an unpredictable individual quirk. In its constant dialogue with words, visualization makes it possible to read not only what words "mean" but also what they cannot convey without supplementation. It makes us see certain visual stimuli while reading; but it also, philosophically, makes us see something of the ways that we read the world.

4

Painters of Reading

"Our fleshly eyes are already much more than receptacles for light rays, colors and lines. . . . They are computers of the world, which have the gift of the visible as it was once said that the inspired man had the gift of tongues."[1] So Maurice Merleau-Ponty asserts in his essay "Eye and Mind," the last piece of work he saw in print before his death. This essay's themes are also those of the philosopher's uncompleted *The Visible and the Invisible*. Eye and mind, visible and invisible, are parallel components of the act of seeing—parallel, too, in the inseparability of the components in each case. The simplistic version of eye and mind has the mind acting as a separate, invisible interpreter of the stimuli sent "inside" from an "outside" objective source. It is not in this sense that eyes are "computers of the world." They do not convey, as if on a terminal, a picture or representation for viewing by the mind—conceived of as a "homunculus" in Stephen Kosslyn's sarcastic jibe.[2] For this is merely to defer the question of the method by which the interpreter interprets. Under the heading of "Blindness (*punctum caecum*) of the 'consciousness,'" one of Merleau-Ponty's working notes for *The Visible and the Invisible* describes what is not seen in the "blind spot" of consciousness: *What* it does not see is what in it prepares the vision of the rest (as the retina is blind at the point where the fibers that will permit the vision spread out into it). *What* it does not see is what makes it see, is its tie to Being, is its corporeity, are the existentials by which the world becomes visible."[3] Seeing takes place *through* a blind spot, both in the eye and in the mind. This may help to explain a paradoxical formulation in Merleau-Ponty's essay: "The proper essence [*le propre*] of the visible is to have a layer [*doublure*] of invisibility in the strict sense, which it makes present as a certain absence" (187). Such paradoxes are a consequence of vision's "corporeity," its embodiment within the world. It would be more comforting, no doubt, to remove ourselves from the body and to view, as if from an Olympian distance, the vectors and ricochets of light rays in a mechanistic model like that of Descartes. But in "Eye and Mind" Merleau-Ponty critiques the Cartesian model at length for ignoring the corporeal situatedness of vision, and of thought about vision: "There is no vision without thought. But *it is not enough* to think in order to see. Vision is a conditioned thought; it is born 'as occasioned' by what happens in the body; it is 'incited' to think by the body" (175). Consequently, at the center of all thinking about vision there must be what Merleau-Ponty calls "a mystery of passivity" akin to the eye's blind spot.

This blind spot may recall Ernst Bloch's "blankness of the now," which prevents us from possessing a world we are too involved with: "We are it itself and are standing too close to it, the spectral and still ineffable nature of consciousness or interiorisation." And indeed Bloch's figure of the forest is refigured in a quotation from the painter André Marchand cited in "Eye and Mind":

In a forest, I have felt many times over that it was not I who looked at the forest. Some days I felt that the trees were looking at me, were speaking to me. . . . I was there, listening. . . . I think that the painter must be penetrated by the universe and not want to penetrate it. . . . I expect to be inwardly submerged, buried. Perhaps I paint to break out. (167)

Here, perhaps, is an example of Merleau-Ponty's "mystery of passivity." The breaking out accomplished when one paints is not simple rebellion or reversal of this: it is the active expression of that mystery of passivity, the act of seeing.

Painting is the subject of "Eye and Mind"; and the ultimate subject of painting, according to Merleau-Ponty, is always visibility itself: "Painting celebrates no other enigma but that of visibility" (166). It makes visible the act of visualizing: "It offers to our *sight* [*regard*], so that it might join with them, the inward traces of vision, and . . . it offers to vision its inward tapestries, the imaginary texture of the real" (165). Inward tapestries—the same weavings that Ashbery celebrates in his poem—take external form in paint. The "traces" spoken of here are not tracings. They are probably closer to the elusive motility of Derrida's use of the term[4] than they are to the idea of a copy or reproduction of an already existent object. In fact, on the previous page Merleau-Ponty explicitly dismisses the idea that the painter's image is "a tracing, a copy, a second thing" and that the mental image is also such a thing (164). Far from being a derivative copy of an external reality, the mental image for Merleau-Ponty spans in one trajectory physical vision and the fantasms of the imagination:

When we say that . . . the phantasm is not observable, that it is empty, non-being, the contrast with the sensible is therefore not absolute. The senses are apparatus to form concretions of the inexhaustible, to form existent significations—But the thing is not really *observable*: there is always a skipping over in every observation, one is never at the thing itself. What we call the *sensible* is only the fact that the indefinite [succession] of *Abschattungen* [shadings] *precipitates*—But, conversely, there is a precipitation or crystallization of the imaginary.[5]

This note for *The Visible and the Invisible* licenses us to take the metaphysic that for Merleau-Ponty characterizes our vision of the actual world and to apply it to our visions of imaginary worlds. And if that metaphysic of vision is the ultimate subject of painting ("Any theory of painting is a metaphysics"),[6] then painting offers a way to learn about the ways that mental images are generated in readers. To paint reading should not be an impossible project.

Certainly writers have conventionally wished that they could call upon painting to express their inner visions. When some striking tableau or moment of scenic grandeur occurs in a nineteenth-century novel, the author promptly laments the limits of literature: Oh, for the skills of a painter! It is purportedly for the sake of the reader's vision that the author wishes for these skills. The reader's vision, however, has a mode of its own; it has been active before these overtly pictorial moments, and in ways that are other than those of representational painting. Nineteenth-century authors have indeed presented us with widely divergent ideas of how readers visualize.

At one end of the continuum we have the inchoate visuality described by Walter Pater in his "Apollo in Picardy": "Soft wintry auroras seemed to play behind whole pages of crabbed textual writing, line and figure bending, breathing, flaming, into lovely 'arrangements' that were like music made visible."[7] Here Pater considers an ineffable play "behind" the graphic sign, and other than it—visual in a way that is not pictorial. This visuality he can express only through another art, that of music. And this reference to music "made visible" paradoxically causes the visual stimulus of the text to become more ethereal, closer to invisibility.

At the opposite end of the continuum we find the kind of fully realized and all-absorbing spectacle described in Charlotte Brontë's *Shirley*:

> He reads: he is led into a solitary mountain region; all round him is rude and desolate, shapeless, and almost colourless. He hears bells tinkle on the wind: forthriding from the formless folds of the mist, dawns on him the brightest vision—a green-robed lady, on a snow-white palfrey; he sees her dress, her gems, and her steed; she arrests him with some mysterious question: he is spell-bound, and must follow her into Fairy-land.[8]

In this apparently opaque word-painting there can be seen a kind of allegory of the process of readerly visualization. The mountain region, no less solitary than the reader's occupation, is far from immediately visible: it is "shapeless, and almost colourless." And it is "formless folds" that give birth to the vision. At the vision's appearance there is an almost gloating itemization of what the reader now "sees." Yet the reader is less a perceiving subject than one subjected to fairy glamour—"spell-bound" by the book, following it into fairyland. Brontë understood this kind of subjection well. At Roe Head School she suffered from hallucinations generated by her own fiction-making activity, in a disconcerting validation of medical warnings about the effect of fiction on female sensibilities.[9]

The paradoxical relations between the visible and the invisible found in these two texts make the subject of their "word-painting"[10] markedly different from that of conventional representation; what is represented is not just an envisioned world but the very process of envisioning. Word-painting becomes the actual painting done by words, the processes by which they cause images to rise in the mind—a subject matter that challenges the painter's resources to their utmost. In "Eye and Mind," Merleau-Ponty considers those resources in turn, even while he warns against equating the effect of painting with any one of them. Nevertheless he finds it worthwhile to consider the effects peculiar to color and line in relation to his metaphysic of vision. I will do the same, with a twist: color and line will be considered in relation to words, and to the images that words can conjure.

Colored Language

Oh that my words were colors! But their tints
May serve perhaps as outlines or slight hints.

Such is Byron's wish in canto 6 of *Don Juan*.[11] His wish seems to have been satisfied, since in the next canto he describes his tale as "a versified aurora borealis" (stanza 2), akin perhaps to those "wintry auroras" that Pater detects playing behind the text. If there is an equivalence between words and colors, every author is a already a painter, beyond any efforts made at mimetic representation; the job of painting reading accordingly becomes an easier one. For Vladimir Nabokov there is no question that such an equivalence exists. In *Speak, Memory*, he gives a long list of color equivalents for the alphabet:

The yellows comprise various *e*'s and *i*'s, creamy *d*, bright-golden *y*, and *u*, whose alphabetical value I can express only by "brassy with an olive sheen." In the brown group, there are the rich rubbery tone of soft *g*, paler *j*, and the drab shoelace of *h*. Finally, among the reds, *b* has the tone called burnt sienna by painters, *m* is a fold of pink flannel, and today I have at last perfectly matched *v* with "Rose Quartz" in Maerz and Paul's *Dictionary of Color*.[12]

From this sensibility emerge such curious statements as that of Adam Krug in *Bend Sinister*, who asserts that "the word 'loyalty' phonetically and visually reminds him of a golden fork lying in the sun on a smooth spread of yellow silk."[13] Imagery like this, for Nabokov, plays subliminally behind his words, in much the same way as the rich and shifting hypnagogic visions to which he was susceptible all his life. So vivid is his inner vision that Nabokov's literary career may be something of a deflection from what nature intended: he is certain that in his earlier years his vocation was to have been a painter.

Nabokov's youthful protagonist in *The Gift* delivers an even more elaborate version of the above passage from Nabokov's memoirs, which enables him to compare himself to Rimbaud. Arthur Rimbaud's "Voyelles" is of course the most notorious attempt to draw an equivalence between words and colors:

A noir, E blanc, I rouge, U vert, O bleu: voyelles,
Je dirai quelque jour vos naissances latentes:
A, noir corset velu des mouches éclatantes
Qui bombinent autour des puanteurs cruelles,

Golfes d'ombre; E, candeurs des vapeurs et des tentes,
Lances des glaciers fiers, rois blancs, frissons d'ombelles;
I, pourpres, sang craché, rire de lèvres belles
Dans la colère ou les ivresses pénitentes;

U, cycles, vibrements divins des mers virides,
Paix des pâtis semés d'animaux, paix des rides
Que l'alchimie imprime aux grands fronts studieux;

O, suprême Clairon plein des strideurs étranges,
Silences traversés des Mondes et des Anges:
— O l'Oméga, rayon violet de Ses Yeux!

A black, E white, I red, U green, O blue: vowels,
I shall one day tell your hidden births:
A, black hairy corselet of bursting flies
that murmur around cruel stenches,

shadowy gulfs; E, candors of mists and of tents,
lances of proud glaciers, white kings, umbels' shiver;
I, purples, spit blood, laughter of fair lips
in anger or in frenzied penitence;

U, cycles, surge divine of glaucous seas,
peace of fields strewn with animals, peace of furrows
that alchemy imprints on large studious brows;

O, supreme Clarion full of strange shrillnesses,
silences traversed by Angels and by Worlds:
— O the Omega, violet light of Its Eyes![14]

Systematic interpretations of Rimbaud's poem have resorted to alchemy, occultism, erotics, and even the lingering effects of a childhood alphabet book.[15] These have delivered no really plausible reading. To accuse the poet of self-indulgent anarchy (or praise him for it) is no more plausible, ignoring the sense of a curious logic as the associations to each vowel spin out metonymically (as Peter Collier suggests)[16] or according to "the law of contrasts" (as James Lawler suggests).[17] The law of contrasts, of course, juxtaposes oppositions within a single vowel's associations—*strideurs* and *silences*, for example—to create a paradoxical effect, an effect that by definition throws into question any framing "law." We are left with a tension between a felt sense of order, akin to those found in dreams, and the impossibility of explicating that sense. We are also left, of course, with the intensity of the visual associations themselves: "The flies, flowers, lips, wrinkles that are put before us are hyperreal fragments without the trace of any supporting fictional or descriptive basis. Such objects are more fascinating than those we know, such feelings and thoughts more acute."[18]

Lawler's reference to fascination suggests more than he probably intended. For Merleau-Ponty, "The painter lives in fascination."[19] No less does the writer, if we recall Maurice Blanchot's words. These involve both the visualized image and its invisible element:

> To write is to let fascination rule language. It is to stay in touch, through language, in language, with the absolute milieu where the thing becomes image again, where the image, instead of alluding to some particular feature, becomes an allusion to the featureless, and instead of a form drawn upon absence, becomes the formless presence of this absence, the opaque, empty opening onto that which is when there is no more world, when there is no world yet.[20]

The apocalyptic tone of Blanchot's closing words chimes with the close of Rimbaud's sonnet. Not only are the images here "groundless figures," as Christopher Collins has described them; the absence of a ground carries over into the paradoxical nature of the images themselves, the continually metamorphosing "presence of this absence," visible manifestation of the invisible. In a final paradoxical twist, all these groundless figures must ultimately evoke the ground out of which they arise—an absent and invisible one.[21] There are, perhaps, certain affinities with hypnagogia. Whatever we call it, it is the source and subject of this poem.

It is not altogether surprising that Rimbaud's sonnet should turn out to be about the paradoxes and powers of visualization. But why should *color*—rather than line, for instance—figure so prominently there, becoming the very source of figuration? One answer might be the large claim said to have been made by Cézanne: that color is "the place where our brain and the universe meet." Merleau-Ponty quotes Cézanne in support of his argument that color is not merely an auxiliary of mimesis; rather, color is "that dimension which creates identities, differences, a texture, a materiality, a something—creates them from itself, for itself."[22] Certainly this describes the feel of the creative force in Rimbaud's poem. A more prosaic explanation is that colors and vowels alike are used by the poet as metonyms for, respectively, visualization and literature. The next section of this chapter will begin by pairing what has been left out of Rimbaud's partial paradigm: not color but line; and not vowels but consonants.

Drawing the Line

In "+R (Into the Bargain)," his essay on the artist Valerio Adami, Derrida asks why one shows drawings. Is it perhaps, he speculates, to "unveil the linear substratum, the intrigue under way, travail in train, the naked *trait* [line, but also characteristic], the traject or stages of a 'journey'? That would be a little simple," he concludes. Of course. Stepping back then, as it were, he exclaims disingenuously, "Without too much arbitrariness, I have just piled up words in *tr*: travail in train, trait, traject, in-trigue [*tramer*]. I could have said tressed, traced, trajectory, traversal, transformation, transcription etc."[23] All this dissemination is then brought home in a bold and perhaps not altogether serious equation:

Let drawing = *tr*

Actually, I suspect, any consonant or consonant cluster would have done here. For *tr* in itself does not have a meaning, Derrida admits; it "only engraves a differential trace. . . . It initiates and breaches [*fraye*] an entirely different body" (174). In marking the difference between one verbal body and another, *tr* divides a certain space of language in a way parallel to the division of the paper's space by drawing, by the drawn line or *trait*. And if we now go on to focus on the line of drawing, this should be done with the awareness that whatever is said of the drawn line may also apply to the written line.

According to Derrida, then, the *trait*, like its initial consonants, initiates by differentiating. However, that differentiation is itself without qualities. Qualities are read into it according to the traces of what it is not, and through the cumulative effect of further *traits*. The line is extended blindly; one is not able to see the vision produced until its production is over. This is the fundamental premise of Derrida's *Memoirs of the Blind*,[24] a premise that is also found in Paul Valéry: "The eye, through its movements on what it sees, must find the path of the pencil on the paper, just as a blind man, by feeling his way, accumulates the elements of contact of a form."[25] It is thus anything but a formal program that gives birth to the drawing's form.[26]

The production of writing proceeds in similar ways. Indeed, "all writing is drawing," according to the title of an essay by Serge Tisseron. "At its origin, graphic expression is blind," he says. "It is guided by muscular, tonic and plastic sensations."[27] Later, it comes to be guided by an internal psychological drama, becoming "a way for the child to stage the mother's coming and going . . . so as to tame and master the experience in the imaginary" (34). For Tisseron, a psychoanalyst, this of course evokes the well-known *fort-da* game that Freud observed his grandson playing. The hand's gesture in both cases throws something out and retrieves it: Piaget has noted the circular repetitive gestures typical of children's earliest drawings. Moreover, the trace of that gesture, the line or *trait*, Tisseron says, "simultaneously separates and binds the pieces of space which it delimits" (34), thus replaying the elements of this primal drama. All of this applies as well to writing: "In writing as well as in drawing, the 'thrown-out gesture' conjures up a trace, a line. This 'line,' which seems tied to his movement, is used by the inscriber to pull back the thought that has been cast out in the act of inscription" (36). The line is separated from the writer, cast into the space of the page; at the same time it may be used to bind that space, to make it the writer's own. The stakes are high and there are no guarantees. The process is often an anxious, tentative one, reflected in the state of the manuscript: scattered phrases, sentences trailing off into ellipses, scratchings-out, scribblings, and (not least significant) doodles—repetitive patterns or interpolated drawings. All these versions of the line are ways of overcoming the writer's anxiety before the empty page, of rehearsing a generative activity whose aim is a fullness of the page that corresponds to a fullness of the self:

In the same way as the child first grasps the imaginary whole of the body upon perceiving himself in the mirror before he realizes its perceptive unity, it is possible that the writer anticipates the imaginary whole of his text, created after the image of his own body as a whole. The outline of his work—or fragments of drafts corresponding to various parts of the project—fulfill, even if they remain incomplete, the function of anticipating fantasmatically the projected totality. (40)

The fantasmatic quality of such anticipations may take a strikingly pictorial form in the manuscripts of novels. When Mervyn Peake must describe the initial encounter of Fuschia and Steerpike in *Titus Groan* (Fig. 3), he resorts *first* to drawing, producing his internal vision in the art he was already known for; words are then tucked in around the edges. The drawing's lines vary in their degree of realization. They are faint near the bottom of the page: two cats' heads are barely indicated, and some lines waver and trail with no clear purpose. But the drawing gains in intensity

FIGURE 3. Mervyn Peake, manuscript page from *Titus Groan*. Reproduced by permission of University College, London, and David Higham Associates, London.

FIGURE 4. Leo Tolstoy, drawing in the holograph of *War and Peace*. From *The Writer's Drawing Book*, ed. Kate Pullinger and Julian Rothenstein. London: Redstone Press, 1994.

as it rises, culminating in the guarded, passionate face of Fuschia. Here we seem to be no longer looking at a surface—of a page or even a face—but at a psychology. Yet even here the mass of dark hair is rendered by repetitive scribbles of the pencil, with no attempt to disguise their texture. Such double effects are common in drawing, of course, and are part of its fascination (in Blanchot's sense of the word). This evolution from sketchy to fully realized, and the doubleness that nevertheless persists, may parallel the process of composition—the way that a visualized scene comes to be embodied in words.

It may also parallel certain effects of reading. For the reader, too, is confronted with a page that, if not blank, is an unknown territory. To make that fictional country one's home, one must first hover over the text, suspending if not disbelief at least precipitate judgment; then, gradually, hints scattered in the spatiality of the text are combined or combine themselves in the mind. Finally a certain "body" makes itself apparent, whether this be a body of significance or a bodied image, or both. A page from the manuscript of *War and Peace* (Fig. 4) suggests this process. The drawn figures seem to be behind the words, seen through them; only in one place does a head clearly emerge from the text, which seems to pull back for it.[28] The logical explanation is that the drawing was made first, like Peake's, and then overwritten. The psychological effect, though, is to see the image as *within* the lines of the text, and in the course of emerging through them—rather like the ghost that lurks faintly behind the pattern of Charlotte Perkins Gilman's yellow wallpaper. Such examples signal—to use Claude Gandelman's words about the sketches of Proust—"the eruption of phantasms into the narrative as the origin and foundation of the novel itself."[29] And these foundational fantasms are as characteristic of the reader's experience as of the author's.

Three Artists' Books

In what ways, then, can artists represent the reader's experience? Certainly not by a mere depiction of what is visualized; there must be a simultaneity, a doubleness, a sense of what the image has risen out of (visible print) as well as the visualized image. This art will be characterized by double exposures, visual puns or paradoxes; it will shuttle between letter and image, material and immaterial, visible and invisible. To illustrate the range of possible realizations I will use work by Roland Sabatier, Tom Phillips, and Jan Sawka.

An art that moves in this range need not always be friendly to what has been called the "mirage effect."[30] The French movement known as *Lettrisme* is meant to make us aware of the nature of signs—their capacity to be combined in aesthetic patterns independent of "meaning," let alone of mirages. Yet if Lettrists are indifferent or hostile to readerly visualization, they do foreground the visual nature of the letters they use; often these are pictorial in nature, rebuses or hieroglyphics or merely drawings substituted for nouns. Such techniques implicitly dramatize the problem of the visual and the verbal, the visual *in* the verbal.

As an example, take one page from Roland Sabatier's 1991 novel *Auparavant* (Fig. 5). In his prefatory note, Sabatier presents his novel as "a hypergraphic narration, founded on the unified reunion of all possible forms of notation and writing." *Hypergraphic* is one of those terms generated at intervals by manifestos, less important as a word than in the ways it is defined, and less important as it is defined than as it is realized in specific works. In "Qu'est-ce que la lettrisme?" Maurice Lemaître defines hyper-

FIGURE 5. Roland Sabatier, page from *Auparavant*.
Paris: Editions Voix Richard Meier, 1991.

graphics as an "ensemble of signs capable of transmitting the reality served
by the consciousness more exactly than all the former fragmentary and partial practices (phonetic alphabets, algebra, geometry, painting, music, and
so forth)."[31] If we now look at Sabatier's page we find many of these fragmentary practices, and others: representational drawings, crude runes,
something like Braille, a musical note, a geometrical figure, mirror writing.
A prominent place is given (as in other Lettrist works) to rebus; among
other reasons for its prominence, rebus may remind us of Freud's trust in
that system as a way of reading the unconscious. Here, the rebus material
within the speech balloon can be deciphered as

> Voici un pied ou est l'autre? C'est un drôle de découpage.

> Here is one foot where is the other? It's a comic cutout.

—and indeed the figure saying these words is cut off at the knees. Significantly, the rules of rebus—which involve visual/verbal punning—are broken here by the "foot," which is simple picture-writing. The page as a whole defies interpretive consistency: the system of signs is constantly shifting, refusing to abide by the rules. In those instances, such as the speech balloon, where we succeed in arriving at the "meaning," the game turns out not to be worth the candle. The point of this "game," however, is not any meaning transmitted by it, but the nature of the signifying game itself. What is to be transmitted, Lemaître says, is "the reality served by the consciousness"—and we should note the position of consciousness here, subjected to a reality that is wholly a signifying system. So complete is this subjection that Sabatier, in his preface, admits that he is subjected, too, as is his work. This avant-garde novel can never realize itself as such because it must always be read in terms of earlier work if it is to be read at all. It is thus impossible to go beyond the "before," the ever-anticipatory *auparavant*.

Yet despite its insistence on the surface of the page, Lettrism occasionally depicts something beyond it: in one page from *Amos*, a work by the movement's leader, Jean Isidore Isou, a man's face emerges behind a scrim of signs (Fig. 6), rather as in the Tolstoy drawing. Indeed, the very fact that Sabatier's work is cast in the format of a novel comments on the way we have read novels before this, reminding us that some kind of "visual eloquence," as he calls it, was always a component of reading.

The novel format, and the critique it implies, plays a much larger part in *A Humument*, by Tom Phillips, which is actually painted on the pages of an earlier novel. The book began in 1966 when Phillips read an interview with William Burroughs in the *Paris Review* and learned about his cut-up texts. Intrigued, Phillips decided to produce a "treated" novel, on two conditions: the novel to be treated could not cost more than threepence; and the project could be worked on only in the evenings, so as not to take time from more important projects. The first condition was fulfilled when Phillips found, for exactly threepence, an 1892 edition of William Hurrell Mallock's *A Human Document*. The second condition was transgressed as the project moved from a piece of play at the fringes of Phillips's days into the obsession of a lifetime.

A Human Document changed its title to *A Humument* when Phillips folded the page under and read the new running head. At the sides of the page, following Burroughs's lead, he first looked for "column edge" poems.

FIGURE 6. Jean Isidore Isou, *Amos, ou introduction à la métagraphologie.* Paris: Arcanes, 1952.

Words not in the poem were painted over, often following the contours of the print's disposition on the page.

Soon Phillips moved in from the margins to connect more clusters and strings of words. These connections were made explicit by outlining the rivulets of blankness that run between words—thus forming strings and balloons sometimes reminiscent of comic-strip conventions, at other times of Celtic interlace. Generally abstract, these sinuous wavering lines may occasionally be used for representation; when this is done, the image takes on a distinctive outline from being determined by these chance meanderings between print.

The conventionally absent and formless ground thus becomes form. At the same time a new content emerges: "That which he hid I reveal," Phillips announces on the first page of *A Humument*. He subverts Mallock's story, tinged with anti-Semitism and conservatism, of a prolonged and painfully honorable love affair at a fashionable European spa; Mallock is now made to speak in voices not his own. On a page that has been overpainted with a portrait of Mallock, the surviving text reads: "He happened to be taking from his pocket, a small photograph of an ancient English lover / a certain part of the lover was rigid." Sly erotica like this one appear throughout Phillips's book, along with comments on the state of art in England; autobiographical references; many musical passages, including the germ of an entire opera, *Irma*; and a "Progress of Love" markedly different from Mallock's original, having as its protagonist one Bill Toge, whose story can be told only in pages on which the words "together" or "altogether" appear. Finally there are what Phillips has called "surrealist catastrophes"—curious pieces of found poetry extracted like fossils from the escarpment of the page. Besides all this variety there is the variety of Phillips's treatment of pages—a virtuoso display of techniques, tones, and textures.

Yet all this, we must remember, is held within a *book*—a book that is held in the hand and whose pages are turned in a physical experience that is both like and unlike the usual experience of reading. Often the text can be read through the scrim of Phillips's treatment of it. Indeed, in each of the pages the physicality of print reminds us of the page that underlies this page. As in Hemingway, "the thing left out" returns all the more forcibly for having been repressed: beyond its richly varied commentary, *A Humument* is always saying something about the nature of the book. At first it may appear that Phillips is saying something that's already been said. "One kind of impulse that brought this book into slow being," he tells us, "was the prevailing climate of textual criticism. As a text, *A Humument* is not unaware of what then occupied the pages of *Tel Quel*."[32] Thus Phillips can describe his book as simultaneously a structuralist *bricolage* and as "a massive *déconstruction* job" done on Mallock's book. Odd bedfellows—but what is demonstrated both by putting together and by taking apart is the idea that the sign has no necessary and originary connection to "meaning."

In this respect Phillips has affinities with the Lettrists. Still, Phillips's transformation of the text from literal to visual often reminds us of a certain activity "beyond" the text. Reading, after all, never takes place *in* the text (wherever that dubious location may be) but always *around* the text in a kind of periconsciousness—what flickers at the edges of the mind while reading. The edges of the mind, of course, are the very country where "surrealist catastrophes" take place. So Phillips gives us a page where everything is occluded except for the line "Then he closed his book; and his mind, with an odd rapidity,"—the sentence is finished by the shapes below. These shapes scrupulously follow the contours of an inset poem, with its inlets of white eating into the squared-off stanzas; they suggest something of what happens to print when it has left the book for the mind of the reader. Not images, perhaps, but not print either—a disconcerting sense of mutation and motion, "an odd rapidity."

When books are depicted in Phillips's book—as they repeatedly are—the depiction is done in such a way as to imply the imaging process generated by reading. One page (Fig. 7) shows a book that has been opened. The left page of this book is an abstract rendering of print as vaguely runic, colored, and complexly layered. Facing this page is one containing three illustrations, as well as a torrential shape possibly emerging from them; or else it is raising itself up in front of them, a dim face emerging, a billowy arm beckoning. In any case, the shape is compounded of the same tones and textures as the illustrations. What is implied by this page and others in the book is the tendency of a material page to generate immaterial images.

Still, a nagging voice argues that Phillips's techniques emphasize the book as a material matrix of possibilities. That voice was mine once, speaking to Phillips himself. "I tend to read your book in terms of the page's translucency," I said, "whereas . . ." As I hesitated, he finished my sentence: "Whereas what I do is to occlude the page. Still, it's been pointed out to

FIGURE 7. Tom Phillips, page from *A Humument*. London: Thames & Hudson, 1987. Copyright © Tom Phillips 1998 / VIS*ART Copyright Inc.

me that *A Humument* is full of windows." Through the phrase "it's been pointed out to me," Phillips acknowledged that any work of stature must have more and other meanings than those its maker intended. Not that Phillips "intends" in any rigid sense: one of the pages of *A Humument* reads "His aim was not to think his aim." The many windows depicted in *A Humument*, then, may be magic casements, opening onto a poetics of reading characterized by illusionism, visual stimuli, and dream reading— for one page even tells us "I am the window your dream stepped out of." And we recall that when Italo Calvino describes the initiatory moments of a novel, he begins with a window: "There is someone looking through the befogged glass." The vision of the reader seeks something that begins to appear only cloudily, like that cloudy shape we have seen rendered on Phillips's page. Phillips thus creates an art of double exposure (and at times double cross). While never letting us forget the material fact of print on the page, he also reminds us that the page can produce colors, shapes, and textures. As his transformed pages accumulate to correspond exactly to the number of pages in Mallock's original novel, they comment, with visual eloquence, on the transformative power of any novel.

That power is the explicit subject of Jan Sawka's *A Book of Fiction*. In his preface, Sawka announces that his book is about the "translation of written images into visual ones"; it is the process of translation, rather than its product, that intrigues him. His book consists of five chapters of five pages each, closely inscribed with a wholly imaginary language. These pages are overlaid with images, or they open up "into" these images; it is sometimes difficult to tell which is the case. Yet there is nothing vague or fuzzy about Sawka's vision: his colors are usually intense and pulsating, his lines meticulously engraved. While not illustrating any particular narrative, the pages convey a certain sense of narrative progression. The first page of chapter 1, for instance, seems to be about the establishment of the novel's protagonist. Where an illuminated initial might ordinarily appear, we have the depiction of a man's trousered feet, casting a shadow before them. Dominating the page is a cluster of images of different sizes, some framed, all seeming to exchange certain elements of color or line or subject matter; above all we see a large shadowy male head, whose sunglasses reflect a distant horizon; this scene of the horizon is repeated in a long band below. The implied question is whether we can "see" anything in a novel without at the same time seeing the one doing the seeing.

A Book of Fiction expresses the feel of reading through a variety of techniques: scattered, framed, and numbered vignettes that correspond, perhaps, to the stage at which the reader is still assembling scattered hints; arrows, diagrams, and geometrical correspondences as equivalents of sensed structures; windows and doors in the page as openings into illusion; and a persistent ambiguity as to what is in "front" of the page and what is "behind" it. Let's linger on one page (Fig. 8), the opening page of chapter 3.

James Beck, in a forward to the book, describes the scene depicted here as "a landscape with two rows of trees lying on a freshly plowed field; expanding branches block out the sky."[33] But the representation is more problematic than this. What Beck reads as furrows seem rather to be serried cutouts, with the trees expanding to wide bases, one behind the other. At the same time, these are illuminated at edges that seem to curve. The illumination appears to be moonlight; yet there is a band of intense rose and white at the horizon. Is the darkness above the tree branches, then, a lowering cloud cover? Its upper edge, though, is rendered almost as if it were shadowy foliage. The complicated interlace of the branches, the repetitive rows of trees leading us into the distance—these parallel and perhaps comment on the equally complicated interlace of writing above. As in the conclusion of Calvino's *The Baron in the Trees*, writing is like a forest, and a forest is like writing, writing that is also drawing. Here we can truly be said to see the forest for the trees; the visualized scene alludes to what generated it. And if what generated it is an interlace of words seen as branches, we sense beyond this the absent ground, the ground that is absence.

Allusive trajectories between what is visualized and the writing that generates it are found throughout *A Book of Fiction*. Serried and repetitive patterns are common in its pages, arising out of patterns inherent in writing: a crowd of men in dark suits, all facing away from us, cast shadows upon the page on which they stand, receding into the distance; mountain ranges overlap parallel with the waves of a sea scene below, and with written lines; purple grasses sprout from the page like sparse calligraphy, and thicken as we move up the page—though not so much that we cannot still detect the rows in which they have been sown; and at "The End," a beach of pebbles, in the foreground sparsely distributed on the sand, recedes into an endless pebbled texture cut across to reveal the top of the written page. In many of the scenes objects emerge out of this complex patterning: a snowy peak rises out of the rounded ranges, an island rises out of the

FIGURE 8. Jan Sawka, page from *A Book of Fiction*. New York: Clarkson N. Potter, 1983. Copyright © 1986 by Jan Sawka. Reprinted by permission of Clarkson N. Potter, Inc., a division of Crown Publishers, Inc.

waves, an intense chartreuse cube rises out of the purple grasses. These too are most likely allusions to Sawka's underlying obsession with the way that a visualized image can emerge out of lines of writing.

Motion / Pictures

A final example of painting reading must occupy a category of its own, creating its effects as it does with the Graphic Paintbox, a computer program. This is Peter Greenaway's *Prospero's Books*, a lushly visual film whose subject is the "magic" of books—a magic which is both figurative and literal. In the second scene of *The Tempest*, Prospero tells of Gonzalo's charity:

> Knowing I loved my books, he furnished me
> From mine own library with volumes that
> I prize above my dukedom. (1.2.166–68)

Greenaway's reading of Shakespeare's play puts these books in the foreground; there are twenty-four of them, each itemized and described in detail. Their descriptions/visualizations[34] make up a variegated argument for the visionary nature of reading. *The Book of Mythologies*, for instance, is a huge volume,

> open and slanted backwards like a raked stage. Sitting and crouching on the double spread of pages—with text and illustrations—are various mythological figures . . . accompanied by nymphs and putti who are endeavoring to turn the next huge page to free the occupants of the next chapter—fauns and hamadryads who are already struggling to get out.[35]

Or take *An Atlas Belonging to Orpheus*, full of maps of hell: "When the atlas is opened the maps bubble with pitch. Avalanches of hot, loose gravel and molten sand fall out of the book to scorch the library floor" (20).

The film catalogs each of these books in turn and immerses the viewer in the reader's visionary experience. The vision of *The Tempest* itself—the experience of the play—arises out of these books. *The Book of Mythologies* is the "template" for the spirits that populate the island. Similarly, *A Book of Architecture and Other Music* operates "like a magnificent pop-up book" whose paper models rise to triumphant music, elaborate themselves, and freeze into a mannerist architectural complex that makes an irony of Prospero's reference to his "poor cell." The books thus create the island and everything that is on it. They also serve as an *ars memoriae*, each book representing a *topos* for the story of Prospero's past as well as the story he now develops. The themes of that story are those of the books: Prospero turns over *The Book of Utopias* as Gonzalo speaks of the ideal society he would create on the island; the altercation with Caliban over the uses of speech is intercut with *The Book of Languages*, out of which "words and sentences and paragraphs gather like black tadpoles or flocking starlings . . . accompanied by a great noise of babbling voices" (96). But the books are not just reminders of or commentary on an already existent story; their powers may be invoked in the writing of new stories. Nowhere in *Prospero's Books* is this point made more spectacularly than in the opening scene.

Prospero is found naked in his bathhouse, standing in a pool surrounded by colonnades. Greenaway describes him as being "like a de la Tour St. Jerome . . . like a Bellini St. Anthony . . . stripped and humbled before a book" (39–40). For on a table beside him in the pool is *The Book of Water*, whose pages have been turned before us in the film's opening shots. Gradually the illustrations have become more animated: at first, the script tells us, only small arrows follow the movement of a diagrammed whirlpool; then at intervals "a wave moves, a ripple-motion animates the drawing of an ebbing tide, animated color sweeps through the black-and-white drawing of a waterfall, a real corpse is buffeted by moving water in an image of the Flood" (39). Out of this book emerges by degrees the full howling tempest that shipwrecks the travelers from Italy.

So Greenaway's film is not only about the powers liberated by reading a book, but also about the powers that are involved in writing one. Prospero is in his bathhouse, but as well—perhaps actually—he is in his study. And as the storm rises in fury he mouths the first word of the play: *Boatswain!* Tentative at first, it becomes a conjuration: the Boatswain is called into being along with the Captain who, in the play, calls for him. His response—"Here Master; what cheer?"—is as much to the master who is Prospero as to the master of the ship. (Later Ariel, explicitly conjured into Prospero's presence, gives a similar reply: "All hail great master, grave sir, hail!") We are given a close-up of the word *Boatswain!* being written: we hear the scratching of the quill, see the ink dry. As Prospero writes the lines of the play he speaks them aloud, "speaking the characters so powerfully through the words," says Greenaway, "that they are conjured before us" (9). The sodden mariners take shape and, in a parallel action, the naked Prospero clothes himself in his cloak, which is also his art. Constantly changing color, it lets escape from its billowing folds a multitude of mythological creatures, along with animals, birds, plants: "The world is in his cloak" (52).

This sense of a tumultuous overspill of power continues as Prospero makes his way to Miranda's bedroom, passing through a long columned hallway crowded with allusive nudes, and then passing through a library scarcely less crowded. "Fantasies," says Foucault, "are carefully deployed in the hushed library, with its columns of books, with its titles aligned on shelves to form a tight enclosure, but within confines that also liberate impossible worlds."[36] So it is with Prospero's library. As he passes through it, each section of the library releases appropriate objects and people. These seem to spill into each other to create Brueghelesque combinations: "Ambiguous bacchanalian figures—wearing birettas and mitres—sit astride a giant abacus. . . . Two giggling nereids—playing with a sheep—swing on a library stepladder. . . . A long-tailed creature sits drinking in the shadow of a tall desk" (52). Such glimpses imply another force of books: their ability to *combine*, forming new books, as in Prospero's library, where the original twenty-four books have begotten thousands more.

The reading of any single book is no less an act of combination, an evolving process that is reflected in the techniques of the Graphic Paintbox. Greenaway begins with print, as any reader must. But that print wavers, perhaps pulses, with color. From behind the scrim of print images then emerge, often revealing more images behind them in a series of translucent planes: "retrospective encasement," Foucault calls this (97). The latter transformations of the text are by no means the dimmest—not in Foucault, not in Greenaway—though they are the furthest from immediate apprehension. Figure and ground give way to each other or function equivocally; semantic and imagistic elements change places in flickering ambiguous ways. Of course, at any moment a visual force may take on strength and focus. Yet no matter how vivid the image may be it is always embedded in the multiple, shifting levels of the reading experience. "Each individual image," according to Wolfgang Iser, "emerges against the background of a past image, which is thereby given its position in the overall continuity, and is also opened up to meanings not apparent when it was first built up."[37] The animation of the text, made visible on Greenaway's screen, arises only

FIGURE 9. Still from Peter Greenaway, *Prospero's Books* (1991).

because the text is itself in motion, in a continual state of process. "Retro-spective encasement" is in this sense also *pro*spective, generative.

The aspect of motion in Greenaway's motion picture would seem to remove it from the works I have analyzed before. Yet for Merleau-Ponty, movement is an essential aspect of painting: "The painting itself would of-fer to my eyes almost the same thing offered them by real movements: a series of appropriately mixed, instantaneous glimpses . . . the outside of a change of place which the spectator would read from the imprint it leaves."[38] Merleau-Ponty's examples in the following pages are drawn from the way that a body in pictorial space can signify physical movement. But his words can be applied equally well to techniques for conveying a move-ment of the mind, or of the mind's eye. For if a print is made of any one frame as Prospero's books are "read" (see Fig. 9), a sense of movement con-tinues to emerge. It emerges through the combining capacities of the Graphic Paintbox, "appropriately mixed" to convey an evolution from one state to another. Glimpses are indeed what we get in Greenaway's shifting image of the book. And what we read in those glimpses is not the book "it-self" but the manner of our reading.

This is no less true of artists like Phillips and Sawka. The amorphous figure of the *Humument* page we have already looked at may be emerging from the depicted book or raising itself up before it. It is in any case moving or evolving out of the tones and textures of the book's illustrations; and the print on the book's facing page seems to be likewise dissolving into tone and texture. Metamorphosis is Phillips's subject here. Similarly, the branching trees of the Sawka illustration, for all their precision and focus, signal a relation to the network of words above them. Even the artifice of the perspective signals a kind of motion in space, perhaps akin to "retrospective encasement." And behind both words and trees the colored page seems to warp and pulse. To read a painting, no less than a page, is to experience motion.

In color, in line, and in their combination by artists to render the reading experience, we have repeatedly found a preoccupation with the invisible forces that generate the visible. For the reader of a novel, of course, "the visible" which is found there must remain invisible to others, and as such might be described as visionary. But if we are to believe Merleau-Ponty, we habitually forget how much of the visual is visionary—though under certain circumstances we may remember what we have forgotten. The painter makes us see not just the physical painting before us but the ways that consciousness sees. The reader enacts this kind of doubleness in an even more paradoxical form, physically seeing words on a page while mentally envisioning visual stimuli. These stimuli may never get past the stage of subliminal pulsations of color or vaguely sensed forms; even the most vividly apprehended mental images are of an order markedly different from that of physical sight. Yet the doubleness of this vision, its complex interpretive negotiations, its presence rising out of a ground that is so elusive as to seem absent—all these may teach us something about physical sight. Such teaching is less involved with specific lessons than with a general heightening of awareness about something familiar to us, which—because it is familiar—is assumed to be already comprehended. The familiarity of vision has rendered it invisible. Painting—in color, in line, and even in words—can make it more visible to the minds where, unrecognized, it has always done its curious work.

5

Framing the Fantasm

"Pictures conjured by text," Peter Greenaway tells us, "can be as tantalizingly substantial as objects and facts and events, constantly framed and re-framed. This framing and re-framing becomes like the text itself—a motif—reminding the viewer that it is all an illusion constantly fitted into a rectangle . . . into a picture frame, a film frame."[1] For Greenaway the pictures conjured up by the reader's visionary eye are "fitted into" a frame in a mode of presentation whose purpose is to remind us that all this is *only* presentation or representation. Yet framing is not just an act that takes place after the picture arises; it is not merely retrospective but prospective. That is, the illusion produced is accomplished *by means of the frame*, broadly defined. What is meant now is not just the rectangle, ornate or simple, within which a picture is contained. We must rather think of all the elements by which the picture is brought into existence—framing in its broader sense of shaping, fashioning, forming. If pictures are conjured by text, that text is not just "like" framing, as Greenaway has it here; text is the frame itself. For a reader vividly to see a scene or character the inner eye requires instruction, as Elaine Scarry has argued.[2] The purpose of these instructions is to produce vision and at the same time to restrain it from overflowing into promiscuously personal associations. And this contradictory nature of the framing text is only the beginning of the paradoxes that attend the idea of the frame.

For Jacques Derrida, the frame is "the decisive structure of what is at stake"[3] in fundamental questions of intrinsic and extrinsic, what is "inside" and what is "outside" the work of art. Derrida makes this claim in the first essay of *The Truth in Painting*, entitled "Parergon." *Parergon* is that which is beside the *ergon* or work; the term is used by Kant in his *Critique of Aesthetic Judgement*. According to Kant, the *parergon* is "only an adjunct, and not an intrinsic constituent in the complete representation of the object. . . . Thus it is with the frames of pictures or the drapery on statues, or the colonnades of palaces."[4] All three of Kant's examples are prominent in Greenaway's film. Colonnades are a favorite architectural motif, invariably framing fantastic forces: they surround the bathhouse in deep perspectives; they make up the long corridor, crowded with the island's spirits, that leads to the library; and they hide within their recesses the visualizations of Prospero's past as he tells his tale. Draperies are at times used as a framing device: huge rich billows of fabric held back by nude bodies, or entwined with them, in the style of seventeenth-century paintings. And Greenaway's nudes—not statues but unabashed flesh—are often accessorized by draperies, sashes, hats, allegorical accoutrements. Finally, the frame itself. It can be as simple here as a floating rectangle of imagery superimposed on the images of the screen's larger rectangle to create a dimensionless line of interface. Or it can be as elaborate as the heavy, ornate frames of the mirrors in which Prospero views his fantasies—these frames themselves framed by the nude bodies that hold up the mirror before him. In all these ways Greenaway gives visual form to the question of the frame.

If the frame is a line between the work's interior and its exterior, it is not, Derrida says, an incisive dividing line, but one that *thickens*:

Parerga have a thickness, a surface which separates them not only (as Kant would have it) from the integral inside, from the body proper of the *ergon*, but also from the outside, from the wall on which the painting is hung, from the space in which statue or column is erected, then, step by step, from the whole field of historical, economic, political inscription in which the drive to signature is produced.[5]

A frame is always within another frame, one that gives meaning to that which is framed, even to the frame itself. This does not mean that we have a series of nested influences which can be neatly labeled. The paradoxes of *ergon/parergon* reproduce themselves within the thickness of every frame.

Derrida speaks of the *passepartout*, the French term for what in English is called a picture's "mat"—a piece of cardboard, of a certain thickness, between the picture, which is seen through the opening cut in it, and the surrounding picture frame. Typically, Derrida plays on the term's multiple meanings: the *passepartout* is a passkey, but it is a key that opens *too much*, for it literally "goes everywhere." Its nature, if we think about it at all, disseminates itself in a series of metaphysical paradoxes, rather than just containing and holding in.

For Derrida, the frame functions as a supplement. It is "half-work and half-outside-the-work, neither work nor outside-the-work and arising in order to supplement it because of the lack within the work" (122). Derrida reiterates a few pages later that the *parergon* "is called in by the hollowing of a certain lacunary quality within the work" (128). Supplementation is made necessary by this hollowness or lack. Yet while listing the frame's parergonal characteristics, Derrida has also said that it is "indispensable to *energeia* in order to liberate surplus value by enclosing labor" (71). Here the frame is associated not with lack but with "surplus." And the surplus is that of *energeia*. This classic rhetorical term, in contrast to the *parergon*, refers to that which is "in" the work or ergon. It is also what is *at* work: both Aristotle and Quintilian stress the term's connection to activity, action. For Aristotle *energeia* shows things "in a state of activity" and is achieved "by putting things directly before the eyes of the audience."[6] This idea of the term moves it closer to what Quintilian would call *enargeia* (the base word here is not *ergon* but *argos*, meaning "bright" or "shining"), the quality in rhetoric that displays things "in their living truth to the eyes of the mind."[7] All this enables us to see, implicit in Derrida's ideas of framing, not only the paradoxes of within/without that he habitually works with, but another, less familiar paradox. The framing process that is necessary to the creation of any work implies at the same time two very different things. On the one hand: lack, lacuna, hollowness, emptiness. On the other hand: energy, vividness, image, and excess of image. The frame of reading operates with and between these oppositions. Though reading is not framed in the same way that a painting is, it is nothing if not a series of complex framing acts, whose components are such things as letters, words, conventions, repetitions, interpretations, and readerly predispositions. *The Truth in Painting*, rightly used, can then teach us something as well about the truth in reading.

Coleridge's Circles

I will frame my argument in terms of Coleridge's great and elusive poem "Kubla Khan," which is almost entirely made up of multiple frames. The first of these are the poem's titles, which belong to what Gérard Genette would call the "peritext," a textual equivalent of Derrida's Kantian *parergon*.[8] There are actually three titles:

Kubla Khan

OR, A VISION IN A DREAM

A FRAGMENT

The vague exoticism of the first title is misleading in that it promises an account of a person rather than a place: whatever the poem that follows is about, its subject is certainly not Kubla Khan. This first title is supplemented through the conventional "or" introducing a title that neither replaces nor retains its predecessor, but rather alternates with it. In a sense it alternates within itself: the dream vision, a common enough genre, often includes a tension between the unmediated "vision" and the delusory possibilities of "dream." Here the tension is contained in a framed relationship with vision *inside* of dream. Finally "A Fragment" supplements both preceding titles. It sets up another tension with the implied full revelation of "vision," while adding another term in the series of recessive frames: a fragment of a vision in a dream.

The prefatory account of the work's invention, which Elizabeth Schneider has shown to be largely a fiction,[9] also functions as a frame. It provides information unavailable from the work itself, information that influences what the work may become in the reader's eyes. The account appears at first merely to extend the notion of a psychological curiosity with the explicit mention of opium. But through the person from Porlock is introduced, perhaps, an allegorical tension between full Romantic vision and the Wordsworthian "glimpses" (or Coleridgean shortfall) that we must content ourselves with as the business of living continues to call us back to the quotidian. Even before it begins, then, the work is already being framed in a certain way, and the effects of that framing are as much a part of the "inside" as of the "outside" of the work.

Within the prefatory account of this fragment is embedded a fragment from another whole: ten lines from Coleridge's "The Picture; or, The

Lover's Resolution." These are framed by the anecdote so that they become a simile (itself perhaps a way of framing)[10] for the loss of vision experienced after speaking with the person from Porlock: "With the exception of some eight or ten scattered lines and images, all the rest had passed away like the images on the surface of a stream into which a stone has been cast, but alas! without the after restoration of the latter!" After this comment follow these lines:

> Then all the charm
> Is broken—all that phantom world so fair
> Vanishes, and a thousand circlets spread,
> And each mis-shape[s] the other. Stay awhile,
> Poor youth! who scarcely dar'st lift up thine eyes—
> The stream will soon renew its smoothness, soon
> The visions will return! And lo, he stays,
> And soon the fragments dim of lovely forms
> Come trembling back, unite, and now once more
> The pool becomes a mirror.

The use of this excerpt raises questions similar to those generically raised by the epigraph, another element of peritext. Does the epigraph frame that to which it is affixed? Or is this fragment removed from the context that frames it and then bent to its user's purpose, fit into a new frame?[11] In the case of Coleridge's quotation from his own poem, there has certainly been distortion of the original; but the quotation in turn bends the new work toward a certain reading: "each mis-shape[s] the other."

Of Coleridge's willed distortions, perhaps the most significant is one that seems trivial: he introduces his lines as if they described the effect of a single stone dropped in water, whereas they really describe a multiplicity of flower heads scattered on the stream. The change allows the lines to correspond more exactly to the single stimulus that is said to be at the poem's origin, the sentence from *Purchas's Pilgrimage*. Viewed in one way, that origin has the solidity of a stone, or a book (the two are of course equated in Wordsworth's dream of the Arab); viewed in another way, it is a hollowing out of the water corresponding to a principle of *lack* in reading. In either case, what is generated is a series of expanding circles within circles, whose embeddedness within one another echoes the peritextual structure we have already analyzed. These circles suggest the expanding transmutations of the original sentence which are now taking place in the mind; they also suggest the expansive action of Coleridge's poem on its reader. If the source of these expanding circles were as multiple as scattered flowers, we would have a view of the poem like that of John Livingstone Lowes in *The Road to Xanadu*, where Coleridge's widespread reading is shown to generate the poem's various images. Instead, the preface encourages us to view the poem as being about the endless generative power of any *single* act of reading.

Reading as Reverie

In the course of his essay on Luther in *The Friend*, Coleridge describes an instance where reading generates hallucination. The scene is in some ways parallel to Foucault's account of St. Anthony's hallucinatory persecution arising out of a book that may be the Bible. In Coleridge's account, too, Luther is reading the Bible, though he is having a difficult time making sense of divine revelation:

O honoured Luther! as easily mightest thou convert the whole City of Rome, with the Pope and the conclave of Cardinals inclusive, as strike a spark of light from the words, and *nothing but words*, of the Alexandrine Version. Disappointed, despondent, enraged, ceasing to *think*, yet continuing his brain on the stretch in solicitation of a thought; and gradually giving himself up to angry fancies, to recollections of past persecutions, to uneasy fears and inward defiances and floating Images of the evil Being, their supposed personal author; he sinks, without perceiving it, into a trance of slumber: during which his brain retains its waking energies, excepting that what would have been mere *thoughts* before, now (the action and counter-weight of his senses and of their impressions being withdrawn) shape and condense themselves into *things*, into realities![12]

At this point Luther has his vision of the devil entering the room he is in—which, in his state between sleeping and waking, he continues to see. He seizes the inkstand and hurls it at his enemy. This incident, with its curious merging of dream and reality, is of interest to Coleridge in the context of his ongoing speculation on hallucinations, optical illusions, and apparitions—and the relation of all these modes of perception to the processes by which we create "reality." But it is also apparent that the passage just cited is in many ways congruent with the prefatory statement describing the genesis of "Kubla Khan," which also begins with the page's black and

white. A particular *kind* of hallucination is thus suggested, the kind produced by reading.

Through a number of authors we know Coleridge to have read, he
had become familiar with an eighteenth-century concept of reading as
reverie, which stresses above all the text's ability to generate visual stimuli.[13]
Erasmus Darwin, in his *Zoonomia* (1794–96), included a chapter on reverie that asserted it to be the distinctive state produced by a deeply absorb-
ing book; and he continued to develop this idea in the dialogues between
Poet and Bookseller that form the Interludes of *The Loves of the Plants*.[14] If,
absorbed by the fictional world, we cease to attend to the external world
and suspend our faculties of judgment and comparison, "a complete reverie is produced; during which time . . . the objects themselves appear to
exist before us. This, I think, has been called by an ingenious critic 'the
ideal presence' of such objects."[15] The "ingenious critic" is Lord Kames,
who, in his *Elements of Criticism* (1762) had spoken of

the pleasure that is felt in a reverie, where a man, losing sight of himself, is totally
occupied with the objects passing in his mind, which he conceives to be really ex-
isting in his presence. The power of speech to raise emotions depends entirely on
the artifice of raising such lively and distinct images as are here described. The
reader's passions are never sensibly moved, till he be thrown into a kind of reverie;
in which state, losing the consciousness of self, and of reading, his present occupation, he conceives every incident as passing in his presence, precisely as if he
were an eye-witness.[16]

Not *precisely* that, indicates Archibald Alison thirty years later in his *Essays
on the Nature and Principles of Taste* (1790). He too believes that the passions are moved only "when we lose ourselves among the number of images that pass before our minds," which he describes as "a romantic
dream." However, the object imaged by the reader cannot be of the same
order as that presented by the visual stimulus of a real object: a reader's image "can have but a very distant relation to the object."[17] Moreover, the
reader's images need not be the literal enactment of those described in the
text, for "the object itself appears only to serve as a hint, to awaken the
imagination" (40). Both because the reader's image is of a different order
from real images, and because that image may generate others remote from
the text's descriptions, "we are conscious of a variety of images in our
minds very different from those which the objects themselves can present
to the eye" (18). We revel in this visual difference, and in the page's ability

to generate it in such variety, a surplus that nearly obliterates the page: "There are times [when] the first lines we meet with take possession of the imagination, and awaken in it such innumerable trains of fancy, as almost leave behind the fancy of the poet" (20).

Alison is both complimented and dismissed by Coleridge in his essay "On the Principles of Genial Criticism": "In explaining by the laws of association the effects produced on the spectator by such and such impressions . . . as in Alison, &c, much has been said well and truly; but the principle itself is too vague for practical guidance."[18] Coleridge's criticism of associationism (and thus of such associationist critics as Kames and Alison) belongs, however, to a later period than the one during which the writing of "Kubla Khan" can be at least approximately fixed—1797, most likely, and no later than 1800. The year 1801 still saw Coleridge coupling Hartley's name with Newton's only a few months before announcing the overthrow of associationism in a letter written in March.[19] And the strand of associationist thinking having to do with reading was not so easily extricated from Coleridge's mind. As late as 1818, lecturing on *The Tempest*, Coleridge asserted, "Our state while we are dreaming differs from that in which we are in the perusal of a deeply interesting Novel, in the degree rather than in the Kind."[20] In the context of these theories of reading, Coleridge's choice of words in his note to the Marquis of Crewe becomes significant: "Kubla Khan," he says, was "composed in a sort of Reverie."

My use of these words, however, is open to a natural objection: their subject is not reading but composition. In the original prefatory note to "Kubla Khan" the two activities (if we accept the hallucinations as produced by reading) are paralleled. The images rise up before the mind "with a parallel production of the correspondent expressions, without any sensation or consciousness of effort." What is implied, then, is the interdependence of writing and reading, which are not neatly separable into productive and receptive acts. In a sense, each frames the other. Reading is always a form of co-writing, as Gaston Bachelard has pointed out: "The joy of reading appears to be the reflection of the joy of writing, as though the reader were the writer's ghost."[21] And writing, on those occasions when it *is* joyful, can be seen the way Blake sees it, as the act of taking from dictation the words of a ghostly presence: "I have written this Poem from immediate Dictation, twelve or sometimes twenty or thirty lines at a time, without Premeditation & even against my Will."[22] So inspiration, "without any sensation or consciousness of effort," is like reading an already written text. And this way of conceiving writing may also involve the generation of fantasmatic images. John Gardner tells of a hallucinatory experience that followed a three-day writing binge:

> As I sat, passive, it came to me that the room was full of a mumble of voices much like the mumble one hears as one slips into dreams, except much louder, as loud as the voices at an ordinary, crowded party; and the room was full, too, of obscure shapes, forms as large and solid as bears or people but unstable: by the slightest effort I could change them into anything or anyone I pleased. All this surprised me but did not at all stir fear or anxiety, because what was happening seemed clear— in fact, I seemed to recognize the experience. While I was writing, earlier, I had been daydreaming similar creatures and voices. . . . Now, as the controlling intellect relaxed, the darker machinery was running overtime, without purpose, filling my room with things not really there.[23]

Traversing Xanadu

The fantasms of "Kubla Khan" are generated equally, then, by reading and by writing. Indeed, what is read is not so much the sentence in *Purchas's Pilgrimage* (which appears only as a *parergon*, as part of the prefatory frame) but writing that is generated by the act of reading, a fantasmatic train of imaged words. So a single sentence gives rise, in Coleridge's mind, to several versions of itself. As in Alison, a line of text generates a train of fancy along its own lines. These lines become literal lines of poetry, which are then read in their turn, generating yet more trains of fancy. The sentence, though in a sense repeated, is never the same twice, becoming dimmer as the productions of the mind increasingly feed off *their* energy rather than that of the sentence which provided the original impetus. In the first section of the poem (lines 1–11) we can still recognize the original sentence from *Purchas's Pilgrimage*, though new elements have been added: the sacred river, the "caverns measureless to man." With the words "But oh!" another train of fancy seems to bounce off the first one, a reactive reading that returns to its source only after sixteen lines, now attaching itself to precisely those elements (the "sacred river," the "caverns measureless to man") that were additions to the original sentence. The reading of the original sentence—amplifying it in the fancy—has now become the writing that is read and amplified in its turn. Beginning at line 31, another wavelike motion of the mind begins, receding in order to advance;[24] it returns to the pleasure dome, gathering it up with fountain and caves, only to have its momentum come to an end six lines later.

In this way the train of images unfolds as each new fantasmatic writing is read in its turn: reading generates writing that is constantly reread and constantly rewritten. Such a movement is like that of the so-called hermeneutic circle. But it may be well to remind ourselves, by way of Derrida reading Hegel, that "this hermeneutic circle has only the (logical, formal, derived) appearance of a vicious circle. It is not a question of escaping from it but on the contrary of engaging in it and going all round it."[25] So we can be urged "not to transgress the law of circle and *pas de cercle* but *trust in them*. Of this trust would thought consist" (33)—including that species of thought we call reading. The expanding circles of "the picture" in the frame may then be reread and consequently rewritten: the mirror on which they play becomes that of reflection, of thought itself. In the reflective medium of water or of the mind, circles are constantly expanding, generating endless surplus. Always beginning again, this movement could be thought of as circular but is also the repeated dissolution of circles. Each single circle is overridden (overwritten) by its successor, and thus passes again into a state of lack.

So it is with the movement of "Kubla Khan." It takes a breath, as it were, and constantly begins again in a recurring *copia*, which is also a series of recurring and increasingly elaborate frames. We never get past those frames. Without shifting directions we find that we are no longer entering but exiting.

At first, the poem seems to consist of a series of preliminaries not just "outside" the poem (titles, prefatory remarks) but "inside" it. For the images of "Kubla Khan," however vivid, are not a satisfying *telos*, and attempts to read the poem symbolically ignore the feeling of narrative *preparation* in this decor. An action seems about to take place in the garden or concerning it—the poem is, in Donald Pearce's words, "teeming with portentousness and a sense of imminent action."[26] We hear "ancestral voices prophesying war." While this may be an echo of actual, Napoleonic war beyond the page, we may also find an incipient war within the symbolical elements of the poem, between chasm and pleasure dome, fountain and cavern, fertile ground and lifeless ocean; yet these remain always and only incipient. Not that they are incapable of being activated in a narration or being reconciled in imagination: only that this is not done. All of the preliminaries end in nothing, passing away "like the images on the surface of a stream." Thus at a certain moment (in the space after line 36), this poem of mounting preliminaries becomes a wistful memory of something lacking.

In a sense, of course, the frame by its nature *aspires* to a certain kind of lack. This lack we have seen before; it is characteristic of the *parergon*. Derrida reminds us that "the *parergon* is a form which has as its traditional determination not that it stands out but that it disappears, buries itself, effaces itself, melts away at the moment it deploys its greatest energy."[27] What *parergon* disappears into, buries itself in, is *ergon*, the work. But *ergon* is created only at the moment that *parergon* "displays its greatest energy." That is to say, the work is generated by multiple framing techniques, which at some moment, a point of "greatest energy," intersect too rapidly and complexly to be separated. Still, we might do well to remind ourselves that this phenomenon has another aspect—that of the *mise en abyme* (a version of the hermeneutic circle), where the frame turns upon itself to contain the act of framing and finds that its source and its end is abyss, that deep romantic chasm.

The only concrete equivalent of abyss at this point in the poem is the blankness after line 36. Judging by what follows, the whole complex vision here dwindles back into that whiteness of the page—and almost immediately begins to expand outward again in a new series of frames. We have, apparently, a new vision of "a damsel with a dulcimer." Framed by the poet's account of her, she in turn frames a vision generated by her artistry. And as we hear more of the poet's desire to revive that artistry and imitate it, it becomes likely that her vision is his vision, the vision we have just lost. Could he revive *her* "symphony," *his* "music" would create familiar pictures: "I would build that dome in air, / That sunny dome! those caves of ice!" All this framing is, then, a revision of the circumstances of vision and loss recounted in the preface, with their order reversed. But there are other differences. The vision is to be replayed now under the tremulous aspect of the conditional—"I *would* build"—which throws into question all that follows, however vivid and exclamatory it may become. And while we are considering such matters of mode we should also consider the smooth transition here from anticipation to retrospection. The vision is something that the speaker hopes to recapture in the future, but when he displays his power most fully it is described by the onlookers as arising out of his past: "For he on honeydew hath fed, / And drunk the milk of Paradise."

The moment of anticipation culminates in a wish or a hope, the conditional line "And all who heard should see them there." Again, words generate fantasmatic images, but now they are quickly elided: the very next line initiates the shift from anticipation to retrospection, and all the more efficiently for its parallelism: "And all should cry, Beware! Beware!" The poet's speech has generated vision in his hearers, which in turn generates speech—but not about that vision. Instead it is the visionary poet, the framer of the vision, who is envisioned: "His flashing eyes, his floating hair!" And this shift from vision itself to a vision of the frame must in turn immediately be contained in frames: "Weave a circle round him thrice."

Blindness and Inner Sight

"And close your eyes with holy dread"—for we cannot look upon the poet, who has generated the vision of that sunny dome, those caves of ice. This line raises yet another way of considering how readerly vision is framed. Closing our eyes before the poet's inspired aspect casts the beholder within, to another source of inspired vision: "My eyes make pictures, when they are shut," begins Coleridge's poem "A Daydream." The source of these pictures remains unknowable, as Coleridge somewhat incoherently confesses: "I have only to shut my eyes to feel how ignorant I am / whence these forms & colored Forms & colors, distinguishable beyond what I can distinguish, these varying & infinitely co-present Colours / these Shapes which I ask what they are / to what they belong in my waking Remembrance—& almost never receive an answer."[28] The paradox of "colours, distinguishable beyond what I can distinguish" implies a contrast between the subtle spectrum intuited by the inner gaze and that limited one distinguished by the waking eye. It is thus the closed eye that sees most and the seeing eye that is blind.

If no source can be found for inner vision, neither is there one for what is externally visible. The eye, be it ever so open, fails to distinguish a "beyond" that could be described as the source of vision or light. "Visibility should—not be visible," Derrida has asserted, explaining that "according to an old, omnipotent logic that has reigned since Plato, that which enables us to see should remain invisible: black, blinding."[29] It is as if one were to stare into the sun, searching for ultimate light and ultimately finding only darkness; or, again, it is like that blind spot in the eye's anatomy that enables seeing to take place. Though visions with closed eyes are no doubt different from what is visible with the eyes open, the difference (like the difference between dreaming and reading) may be one of degree rather than of kind.

Such an argument has been developed by Derrida in his *Memoirs of the Blind*, which originated as the catalog for an exhibit at the Louvre that Derrida was invited to curate. This was the first in a series of such guest-curated exhibits, entitled *Parti Pris* (the second was curated by Peter Greenaway), whose aim was to give to "amateurs" of outstanding abilities in other fields the full resources of the Louvre's collection; this would allow them to form an argument, an original vision in dialogue, as it were, with the museum's artworks. In Derrida's case the vision was about the nature of vision itself, as represented in drawings of the act of seeing by artists, curiously linked to implicit (and sometimes explicit) blindness. And because of a long tradition having to do with blindness, this seeing may be that of the visionary, as well as the physical, eye.

In his book, Derrida speaks of several *traits* of seeing. We recall that the word *trait* in French has two primary meanings: it is a characteristic feature of something, and it is a stroke or line in drawing. Derrida speaks of a trade-off between these two kinds of lines, these different *traits* possessed by him and by a brother gifted at drawing, whose gift he envied. But "I was called by another *trait*, this graphics of invisible words, this accord of time and voice that is called (the) word—or writing, scripture. A substitution, then, a clandestine exchange: one *trait* for another, a *trait* for a *trait*."[30] Here, again, we are encouraged to apply what is said about the graphic line to the written one—which we note is not without a graphic component, a "graphics of invisible words."

Derrida discusses three aspects of the *trait*. The first of these is the blindness involved in drawing the line:

In the *tracing* potency of the *trait*, at the instant when the point at the point of the hand . . . moves forward upon making contact with the surface, the inscription of the inscribable is not seen. Whether it be improvised or not, the invention of the *trait* does not follow, it does not conform to what is presently visible, to what would be set in front of me as a theme.[31]

That this may apply not only to the artist's line but also to the writer's is demonstrated by an entry in Coleridge's notebooks, an entry that describes the point of contact with the page as writing moves forward: "Dec. 28, 1803—Beautiful luminous Shadow of my pencil point following it from the Candle—rather going before it & illuminating the word, I am writing"[32] Jerome Christensen lingers on the comma, asking whether the last phrase is a restrictive clause or whether we should stop before the statement that sums up the activity in which Coleridge is engaged.[33] In either case, the implications remain the same, implications about writing as a process generated word by word. It is described here as a paradoxical process. The shadow illuminates; that which blocks visibility illuminates the word. There are links here to the idea of closing one's eyes to see the pictures that are generated there; and to the seeing generated by reading, which obliterates the visible page.[34] There is also, perhaps, a link to the "illuminating" of the word practiced by medieval scribes, where the contours of the letter—meant to be read for its "spirit" and therefore to be invisible to the bodily eye—take on the life of lines in drawing, even to the point of generating fantastic burgeoning visions: ornament becoming animal, vegetable, human by turns or even simultaneously, monstrous combinations springing as much from the fancy of the scribe as from the willful line on the page. We recall the fantastic visions of St. Anthony and Luther, who embellish in this way even the Word. The light of revelation may thus be illuminated with the shadowy shapes that populate the brains of its readers. And for the writer, it is these shadowy shapes that shape the words. The very contact of pen to paper here causes a faint path to stretch out—Derrida speaks of the *trait*'s "originary, pathbreaking [*frayage*] moment" (*Memoirs of the Blind*, 45), as he has earlier spoken of "what always guides writing through the night, *farther* or *no farther* [*plus loin*] than the seeable or the foreseeable," adding: "'*Plus loin*' can here mean either excess or lack" (4). Writing is guided by a shadowy anticipation, then, which may be thought of as reading what is not yet on the page. These are Derrida's "graphics of the invisible words" with a vengeance—and not unrelated, perhaps, to Coleridge's "forms & colored Forms & colors, distinguishable beyond what I can distinguish."

Once the line is fixed on the page the same sort of process continues. Derrida's second aspect of the *trait* deals with how it is read after being committed to paper:

A tracing, an outline, cannot be seen. One should in fact not see it . . . insofar as all the colored thickness that it retains tends to wear itself out so as to mark the single edge of a contour: between the inside and the outside of a figure. Once this limit is reached, there is nothing more to see, not even black and white, not even figure/form, and this is the *trait*, this is the line itself: which is thus no longer what it is, because from then on it never relates to itself without dividing itself just as soon, the divisibility of the *trait* here interrupting all pure identification. . . . Drawing always signals toward this inaccessibility, toward the threshold where only the surroundings of the *trait* appear—that which the *trait* spaces by delimiting and which thus does not belong to the *trait*. (53–54)

We can read the *trait* here in terms of the paradoxes of frame—are encouraged to do so by Derrida's language. On the one hand, only the "surroundings" of the *trait* appear, thus appearing to frame it; on the other hand (though presented as an appositive), we have "that which the *trait* spaces by delimiting," which is thus framed by the *trait*. Is the *trait* surrounded, then, or does it surround, delimit? Both, no doubt, and this is true in writing as well as in drawing. The *trait* is necessary to call the framing process into being on the blank paper, but then is framed, assigned a significance, read by a process that is not just a matter of what is on the paper's surface. We may call that process projective or, more dramatically, hallucinatory; but it does not operate in emptiness. It cannot operate without first fastening on a *trait*. Coleridge, somewhat like Luther, thought he saw an apparition sitting across from him in his library—an apparition that resolved itself into a complex play between his mental "substratum" and the optically distorted shape of a port flask.[35] Did the flask's shape cause him to frame it as a man? Or did his thoughts of the man frame the flask until it took on that optical semblance? These questions circle each other in a movement which reproduces that of the most fundamental questions of reading.

The final aspect considered by Derrida is what he calls "the rhetoric of the *trait*." The very withdrawal of the drawn line as presence, he argues, is "that which grants speech"—speech that, he has earlier argued, is always implicit in the line of drawing, which though wordless is capable of generating words:

You can hear them resonating all on their own, deep down in the drawing, sometimes right on its skin; because the murmuring of these syllables has already come to well up in it, bits of words parasiting it and producing interference; and in order to perceive this haunting one need only abandon oneself to the ghosts of discourse by closing one's eyes. (39)

"The ghosts of discourse"—we may play with this phrase in the same way that Derrida likes to. It may be seen as referring not only to traces of discourse in drawing, but also to that which haunts discourse itself: traces of the visual, the "graphics of invisible words." Words evoked by pictures, pictures evoked by words—"each the other's difference bears," to reapply a line by Andrew Marvell used by Derrida in another context (129). In both cases, in the case of both *traits*, the work aspires to a kind of haunting. "The very chance of the work," Derrida says, is "the specter of the invisible that the work lets be seen without ever presenting."[36] The paradoxes of this formulation must depend for their resolution upon strategies of frame. Only through the generative power of framing can the "invisible" be "seen"—and moreover "without ever presenting." All that is physically visible are frames, versions of framing—but frames are not all that is to be seen. They are only a means to an end that makes itself up as it goes along, and can never be solidly guaranteed. Thus the work takes a "chance" at conjuring up ("Weave a circle round him thrice") a force that is necessarily apparitional. As for the necessity that generates this vision, to that we are ultimately blind. Just before the passage we are considering Derrida says, "The failure to recapture the presence of the gaze outside of the abyss into which it is sinking is not an accident or weakness; it illustrates or rather figures the very chance of the work, the specter of the invisible." And though these words may have a deconstructive ring to them, they actually concern the very construction of the reader's visionary experience.

Blake's Boxes

This chapter will close, appropriately enough, with an image—though there has been considerable controversy over what the image depicts. "I suppose it to be a Vision," Frederick Tatham has written on the sepia drawing he inherited after the death of Blake's wife (Fig. 10). "Indeed I remember a conversation with Mrs. Blake about it." The conversation, one gathers, did not enlighten him much about William Blake's cryptic scene, which is undated and untitled. Christopher Heppner has suggested that the subject is taken from the second Book of Kings.[37] There we find

FIGURE 10. William Blake, drawing. The Tate Gallery, London. Used by permission.

an account of the prophet Elisha's reception by a woman of Shunem, who says to her husband, "Let us make a little chamber, I pray thee, on the wall; and let us set for him there a bed, and a table, and a stool, and a candle-stick; and it shall be, when he cometh to us, that he shall turn in thither" (4:10). The moment depicted in the drawing, Heppner suggests, is that when the woman is called to Elisha and promised a son. If we are to make the left-hand figure human rather than angelic, as it is often read, it must be stripped of its wings. Actually, we see only one wing, Heppner points out, rereading this shape as a shadow cast upon the wall. I would point out, though, that the angle of the shadow does not correspond to the position of the light, so that the aureole remains to be explained. If the figure—ambiguous to be sure—is divine rather than human, this does not cancel the worth of Heppner's reading: Elisha may still be depicted, even if in communion with angelic rather than human forms. And beyond the biblical subject something may be implied about the nature of the prophet—or of "the inspiration of the poet," the title traditionally assigned to the drawing.

These implications should be sought less within the little enclosed chamber than in the strangely empty space surrounding it. Heppner notes that there is a discrepancy between the vanishing points of the perspectives in the outer and inner chambers. This "interprets and makes visible the relationship between the state of ordinary experience and that of poetic inspiration; the two are closely related and in communion with each other, indeed one is in a sense inside the other, but they are also separated by the profound shift of gears necessary to move between them" (131). Heppner's reading of the drawing's depicted space is the latest in a line of such readings, whose differences are perhaps the most significant thing about them.

Graham Robertson, who acquired the drawing in 1886, described it like this:

The immense room is full of a clear light which penetrates to all corners, and leaves nothing undefined; yet the whole scene is charged with mystery and touched with a remoteness, a loneliness, so intense that we feel that it lies in the land "out of Space, out of Time" where, in the spacious and well-litten Chamber of the Mind, the Poet sits apart in the innermost Holy of Holies, the Shrine of the Imagination, writing wonderful words at Angelic dictation.[38]

In 1969, Robert Rosenblum took a different tack:

At first glance, the convergent perspective lines of the outer and the inner sanctum seem to create two Renaissance box spaces of rudimentary clarity; yet . . . this simplicity is more apparent than real. Thus the shading of the web-like component planes obeys no natural laws, but is manipulated in such a way that the would-be effects of recession are constantly contradicted, producing instead a series of simultaneously convex and concave planes.[39]

Both these descriptions have blind spots. The room is clearly *not* "full of a clear light which penetrates to all corners": the light of the inner room floods across the floor of what should accordingly be a dim outer room—except that the shading, as Rosenblum points out, "obeys no natural laws," any more than do the luminous areas of ceiling and walls. On the other hand, the "convergent perspective lines" noted by Rosenblum do not create a Renaissance-style box. The unnaturally acute angles of the upper lines subvert the idea of a ceiling that recedes in space, tilting it instead so that the convention now reads as a nearly vertical plane—and moreover, as Rosenblum himself says, one that may protrude as easily as it recedes. Rosenblum sees a kinship here with early Cubism's use of shading to create spatial ambiguities. And this kinship, which was certainly unavailable to Blake, emphasizes that Rosenblum, like Robertson before him and Heppner after him, is framing the picture within the chamber of his own mind—as he cannot help doing. Each description then becomes another frame for the picture which in framing it, alters it.

I take my place in this genealogy of descriptions by seeing Blake's drawing as, precisely, a picture about framing. The little scene—human action or conventional iconography of inspiration—dwindles into insignificance before the looming power of what surrounds it. And if we include in those surroundings the blank page that frames the ambiguous room enclosing the inner chamber, then the drawing manifests itself as a receding series of frames. The conventionally representational scene at the bottom of Blake's boxes is read, no matter who does the reading, in terms of its framing: which is the real and undoubted source of the drawing's power, beyond any conventional iconography of creation.

Blake knew the power of the frame. He used it freely, some might even say cavalierly. For anyone thinking of Blake as a seer of eternal verities, it comes as a shock to learn that he often retitled his engravings, adding mottoes or explanatory inscriptions in the borders, and thus making them serve a variety of purposes. In an essay archly entitled "Blake as Humpty Dumpty," Christopher Heppner has analyzed a number of such cases where changes in visual significance are produced by verbal supplementation; he concludes that "the design is a starting point for the activity of producing meaning, rather than a constant containing meaning completed within itself."[40] It is thus the frame that determines the subject; it is not the presumed "truth in painting." In truth, the meaning of the lines on the paper is never wholly determined by those lines, be they ever so wiry and sharp. That sharpness, so necessary to Blake, is the sharpness not of focus but of division—the divisibility of the *trait*, as Derrida would have it—allowing the viewer's inner vision an equal share with what is physically visible on the page, which becomes supplemented in the only process that will produce meaning. "Reason is the bound or outward circumference of Energy," Blake has said in *The Marriage of Heaven and Hell*. It is all too easy to read this as a repressive binding, when in fact the circumference, the bounding line, is what liberates energy or *energeia*, with all its visionary forms. As David Clark has pointed out, citing Blake's words from *Jerusalem*, "'The sanctuary of Eden' lies not in some mysterious centre, but in the equivocal region of the *parerga*: 'in the Camp: in the Outline, / In the Circumference.'"[41]

Blake's equivocal frame, then, so startlingly empty on first glance, pulsates with a strange power; it is both lack and surplus. In contrast, the central scene dwindles to a mere puppet show, puzzling rather than mysterious. Yet perhaps now we may reframe our vision of that scene in small but significant ways. We may notice the marked difference in the quality of the line used to depict the two figures: the heavy, darkly scored lines of the seated figure in contrast to the lighter line of the spectral figure standing beside him—which moreover seems to airily rise in contrast to the downward pull of the seated figure's cloak (or is it a chair back?), melding him into one compact unit with the table at which he is seated. Where he is writing, or drawing, the pen in his right hand resting at the point on the paper where frame expands into vision.

6

A Politics of Visualization

In *Unmarked: The Politics of Performance*, Peggy Phelan argues that there may be a negative side to the demand for visible minorities to be made more visible. Though there is a sense in which such visibility signals acceptance, it is an acceptance in terms of the dominant, and dominating, vision. After all, Phelan mordantly observes, "if representational visibility equals power, then almost-naked young white women should be running Western culture."[1] To be visible is also to be vulnerable—to surveillance, voyeurism, commodification, fetishism, oppression. Above all, the other who is seen can be used as a mirror for the seer's own imaginary, with differences used to shore up the subject's sense of sameness. It is not the object of an act of seeing that matters, then, but the way the subject does the seeing. And here, at the site of the subject, an irrevocable split sunders the purported unity of both seeing and subject. Phelan reminds us of Lacan's comment on the failure of self-seeing: "I am unable to see myself from the place where the Other is looking at me."[2] To compensate for this failure, the other is made to bear the weight of the gaze, affirming the power of the one who wields it: "Until one can accept one's internal other as lost, invisible, an unmarked blank to oneself and within the world, the external other will always bear the marks and scars of the looker's deadening gaze."[3] Not visibility alone, then, but the invisibility that is always a part of the visible must become politicized.

Such a political strategy informs the work of the three artists considered in this chapter: David Wojnarowicz, Derek Jarman, Nicole Brossard. All use their artistry in the service of a queer politics; all do this through an optical critique. That critique is a remarkably unanimous one, though it receives a different emphasis in each artist's work. Together they enact a progression: Wojnarowicz concentrates on dismantling physical vision; Jarman begins with blindness and ends in mental imaging; and Brossard affirms the ways that mental images can take on a dimensioned life in the world. We are shown the degree to which vision is composed of visualization, and how visualization may then recompose our vision and our world. Consciously working behind the scenes of seeing-is-believing vision, these artists remind us of visualization's generative power. Its fantasms are not "mere fantasizing," then, but an active instrument for political change.

Sub-Vision

He was dead of AIDS in 1992 at the age of 38, but in his short intense life David Wojnarowicz created work of significance as a writer, painter, and photographer. Two years after his death, the journal *Aperture*, in an unprecedented move, devoted a whole issue to Wojnarowicz's work; the innovative nature of that work, according to the issue's introduction, "defies traditional concepts of photography, stretching our notions of the medium's possibilities."[4] Well before his death, Wojnarowicz's painting had become lauded and sought after by the New York art world—a development that disgusted him so much that he stopped painting altogether for two years. And finally, in his books *Close to the Knives* and *Memories that Smell like Gasoline*, Wojnarowicz left behind a searingly intense body of writing: influenced by Burroughs and Genet, his style fuses political attack and hallucinatory rapture. Throughout his work, his subject matter is the same: the alienated underbelly of America, the world of the homeless, the hustlers, the faggots and drag queens and drug addicts—and always an incandescent rage at the government's near-genocidal handling of the AIDS epidemic. All this he lived: the chronology of his life is so harrowing that it is hard to see how he survived to 38, quite aside from producing such extraordinary work in three different arts.

Wojnarowicz used each of his arts to push the boundaries of the others, fusing or opposing their languages into one unclassifiable vision. His aim was to dislocate accepted ways of seeing, which he associated with what he called the "pre-invented world," the ready-made ways of seeing into which we are born. In his case, these never had a chance to be absorbed comfortably, and as a result they revealed their coercive and violent side. Wojnarowicz's work became a counterviolence, an imperative to see differently. This "different" seeing, for him, reached its most intense version at the moment of his diagnosis: "The first minute after being diagnosed," he said, "you are forever separated from what you had come to view as your life or living, the world outside the eyes."[5] In questioning the world outside his eyes, or vision itself, he paradoxically becomes an artist whose business it is to strike himself blind.

I want to enter Wojnarowicz's work through his own description, in *Close to the Knives*, of a moment of blindness, a blindness that he *sees*. He has awakened into a blacked-out motel room:

When my eyes first opened it took some measure of time to realize I'd stepped away from myself among the veils of sleep and with that motion my eyes had disconnected from the nerves of the brain: that area where sight flows uninterrupted. The only vision from back there was a sub-vision: the magnified abstraction of a shiny black abdomen like a motorcycle gas tank or a mirrored black globe. Straining against the contours of the room and its furniture to reach back into that area and retrieve more of its form from the shadows, I could see or feel it for moments; the soundless click of its eight legs tapping the surfaces of the walls and ceiling of my sleep.[6]

The imagery is reminiscent of "The Metamorphosis"; one thinks of Kafka's comment that the most dangerous time is the moment of waking, because there is never any guarantee that all the things that make up one's daily life will collect themselves in the same places again. Here nothing collects itself when the eyes open, not even vision. Instead there is a "sub-vision," which might be associated with hypnagogia, often a source of Wojnarowicz's work.[7] More broadly, it can be associated with an inner visualizing whose sources remain unconscious. This subvision is a mode of seeing that is other than physical perception, and yet makes up the largest part of vision. "There is really no difference," Wojnarowicz asserts, "between memory and sight, fantasy and actual vision."[8] Kaja Silverman says much the same thing in *The Threshold of the Visible World*. If she looks at a red chair, "It is not only what transpires between my glance at the red chair and my seemingly instantaneous conscious perception of seeing it which determines what it means in this case to have 'looked.' Before I even register that perception, it has been put into communication with my unconscious memories, and, so, worked over in certain ways."[9] Wojnarowicz's subvision is thus a sub*conscious* vision. This is not to imply that it is inaccessible to conscious sight; on the contrary, the implication is that only the subconscious determines the interpretive significance of retinal stimuli. Wojnarowicz continues: "Vision is made of subtle fragmented movements of the eye. These fragmented pieces of the world are turned and pressed into memory before they can register in the brain. Fantasized images are actually made up of millions of disjointed observations collected and collated into the forms and textures of thought."[10] This seems to be not just theory, but Wojnarowicz's actual experience of seeing: "When I move my eyes very slowly from left to right while sitting still, I can feel and hear a faint clicking sensation suggesting that vision is made up of millions of tiny stills as in transparencies. Since everything is generally in movement around us, then vision is made up of millions of photographed and recalled pieces of information" (53). In other words, I am a camera, and vision is photographic. Yet the image that develops does so in darkness, the camera obscura of the unconscious.

Wojnarowicz's words have stressed the fragmented and disjointed nature of the act of seeing. And this, as he has said elsewhere, "leads to the collage element of the work; it's my experience—I have thousands of these little films or slide transparencies inside my brain; one thing superimposed on top of another."[11] Juxtaposition and superimposition are recurrent techniques in Wojnarowicz's combinatory art. In this he is scarcely unique. But he uses those techniques to produce an uncanny challenge to vision, allowing us in a sense to "see" subvision.

A good example of this is the well-known *Sex Series*: eight photographs all printed in negative, "the queer's X-ray vision," in Lucy Lippard's phrase.[12] Each includes between one and six inset circles, usually depicting sexual acts. The circular insets evoke telescopic or microscopic lenses and are, Wojnarowicz says, about "examination or surveillance."[13] They also seem to punch holes in the depicted scene, exposing visions behind the vision—or they float before the scene like extraterrestrial saucers. In one of the photographs (Fig. 11), a view of Manhattan bridges is overlaid with a relentlessly factual text about government handling of AIDS drugs. The inset circles depict a fetus, an AIDS patient, the National Guard, and a sex act. At the lower right is a saurian figure collaged out of maps, which

FIGURE 11. David Wojnarowicz, from *The Sex Series* (1988–89). Courtesy of the estate of David Wojnarowicz and P.P.O.W., New York.

is swallowing a globe of money; its eyeball is a conventional portrayal of Jesus, its jaws are circled with barbed wire reminiscent of a crown of thorns. At no point can one trust what is outside one's eyes, assert that this is "real" vision. There are only those "slide transparencies" superimposed on one another, their negative state giving them an eerily unreal look. Conventional vision is thus subverted, and subvision installed in its place, if only by implication.

A different technique used to the same end has Wojnarowicz separating out images he might otherwise superimpose in collages; indeed he emphasizes the space between the images, leaving it up to us to create a variety of synaptic connections between them. So a piece called *The Weight of the Earth, Part II* (Fig. 12), consists of fifteen photographs varying in tone and texture; these depict a monumental statue, a drag queen, a frog in a man's hand and a frog being devoured by a snake, the globe of earth in

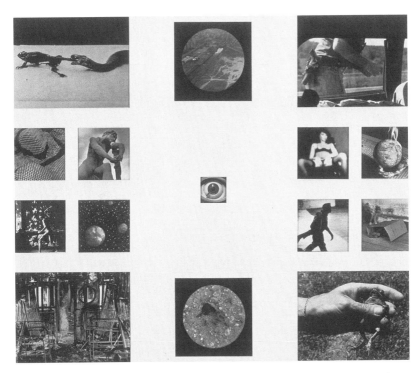

FIGURE 12. David Wojnarowicz, *The Weight of the Earth, Part II* (1988–89). Courtesy of the estate of David Wojnarowicz and P.P.O.W., New York.

space and a toy globe burning, a burned building, the entrance to an ant colony, a man sleeping in a cardboard box, a "monkey man" seen in Java, a naked blindfolded man flailing with a stick, patterned material resembling a topographic grid, a figure with a holstered gun bending outside a car window, an urban long shot. All these surround a staring eye over which an ant crawls. The very representation of seeing, this eye from a carved figure, implies a certain artificiality to vision. The ant crawling over it indicates its deadness, redoubled by the ant's association with a mechanistic social organization. What is to be seen here, then, cannot be trusted to the look alone, but will arise out of the interpretive juxtapositions made *between* the images by each viewer.

Exemplifying two ways of using fragmentation, both of these works could serve as illustrations for a comment by Christian Metz: "The snapshot, like death, is an instantaneous abduction of the object out of the

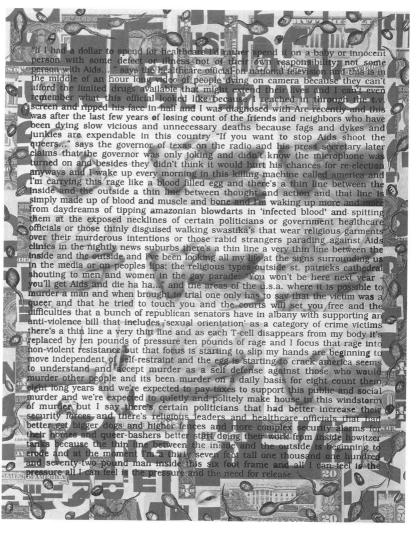

FIGURE 13. David Wojnarowicz, *Untitled* (1988–89). Courtesy of the estate of David Wojnarowicz and P.P.O.W., New York.

world into another world, into another kind of time. . . . It cuts off a piece of [the referent], a fragment, a part object, for a long immobile travel of no return."[14] The journey taken here is out of the preinvented world and into a world which is always in the process of being invented at the level of the unconscious. And what Metz has asserted of the snapshot is also, for Wojnarowicz, true of the word: "I realized," he says, "that photographs were like words in a sentence and that what I try to do is to construct paragraphs out of the multiple images."[15] Looked at in this way, *The Weight of the World, Part II* is a huge paragraph whose referent can never be fixed because it is always developing. Photography, we recall, is etymologically "writing with light."

So Wojnarowicz often superimposes a text over a photographed or painted image, leaving it to us to decide whether the words rise out of the image or the image is evoked by the words. In one untitled work of 1989 (Fig. 13) a text of pure rage against the combination of AIDS neglect and hatred of gays is screened above a series of photographs. The photographs are of Wojnarowicz's friend and mentor Peter Hujar and were taken moments after he died of AIDS complications. Text and images are framed in an intricate composition of letters turned into restless abstractions, interspersed with fragments of money and stylized sperm cut out from maps. The whole is not only a powerful emotional sequence but a commentary on the slippages and alliances between various modes of representation—the representation of gays and AIDS being also a political factor here.

Another use of different modes of representation in one work is *I Feel a Vague Nausea* (Fig. 14), titled after the first words of its text. A few more of those words may underscore points already made:

I feel a vague nausea stroking and tapping the lining of my stomach. The hand holding the burning cigarette travels sideways like a storm cloud drifting over the open desert; how far can I reach? I'm in a car travelling the folds of the southwest region of the country and the road is steadying out and becoming flat and giving off an energy like a vortex leading to the horizon line. I hate arriving at a destination. Transition is always a relief; destination means death to me. If I could figure out a way to remain forever in transition, in the disconnected and unfamiliar, I could remain in a state of perpetual freedom.[16]

These words and more are superimposed over an enormous tropical bloom, sexual in the way that Mapplethorpe's are, and at the same time

FIGURE 14.   David Wojnarowicz, *I Feel a Vague Nausea* (1990). Courtesy of the estate of David Wojnarowicz and P.P.O.W., New York.

partaking of an inhuman sublime. Near the bottom of the painting, five small photographs are stitched on with red string. They are photographs of images in other media, usually in their negative state. All these media set up a restless force field of interactions, leaving the spectator "forever in transition, in the disconnected and unfamiliar." To "make sense" out of the work we must paradoxically go beyond sense, and beyond our senses, into the unconscious dynamics of memory and fantasy.

"Reality" itself, as conventionally opposed to art, becomes only another mode of representation in Wojnarowicz's media collisions. For instance, in the series *Arthur Rimbaud in New York*, Wojnarowicz followed a friend wearing a mask of Rimbaud's face through various aspects of a squalid urban existence: Rimbaud at the diner, Rimbaud dead of an overdose, Rimbaud masturbating, Rimbaud riding the subway, and so on. Wojnarowicz's earliest paintings were stencils of a stylized burning house, applied without comment on the walls of New York City. He then began painting large murals in the rooms of an abandoned warehouse populated after dark by gay men in search of furtive sex. These were throwaway art, not meant for the eyes of the art world—though the art world took notice anyway. One long meditation in *Close to the Knives* has Wojnarowicz passing through this warehouse by night, observing the murals, often erotic, done by him and others, then seeing those murals come to life in fitfully illuminated scenes of sex. Finally he moves past these modes of seeing into the flickering images of subvision:

I thought of the eternal sleep of statues, of marble eyes and lips and the stone wind-blown hair of the rider's horse, of illuminated arms corded with soft unbreathing veins, of the wounding curve of ancient backs stooped for frozen battles, of the ocean and the eyes in fading light, of the white stone warthog in the forest of crowfoot trees, and of the face beneath the sands of the desert still breathing.[17]

Here we may have a source for a photographed self-portrait by Wojnarowicz, where his face, eyes closed and mouth open, is all but buried in crumbling dirt. At first the image seems to depict a burial, but it may also be read as a kind of emergence myth. The image is liminal; like so much of Wojnarowicz's art, it depicts transition without specifying destination. This is what Wojnarowicz has to say about the portrait as a moment of transition:

It's the appearance of a portrait, not the immediate vision I love so much. . . . It's the simple sense of turning slowly, feeling the breath of another body in a quiet room, the stillness shattered by the scraping of a fingernail against a collar line. Turning is the motion that disrupts the vision of fine red and blue lines weaving through the western skies. It is the motion that sets into trembling the subtle water-movements of shadows, like lines following the disappearance of a man beneath the surface of an abandoned lake. (9–10)

The final image may echo the drowned man from book 5 of *The Prelude*, and the recurrent "lines" might then allude to those in the books whose liminality is Wordsworth's subject. Or the image may be the enactment in a watery medium of Wojnarowicz's ambiguous self-portrait. In either case, this passage begins with appearance, ends with disappearance, and blurs the distinction between them. Precisely between is the moment of turning. To understand why "turning is the motion that disrupts the vision" we must realize that the Renaissance perspective system depends entirely on a fixed viewpoint. As soon as the viewer moves or turns, the field of vision flows, warps, distorts—we are made aware that we are not outside the visual field looking dispassionately into it as into a box. We inhabit the same space as the objects viewed, and our motions continually disrupt that space, modifying it and our vision.

The title of the essay from which this passage comes is "Losing the Form in Darkness." It is no less true, though, that darkness is where the form may be found—whether that form is the sexual male body or the hallucinatory-hypnagogic images thrown up by the unconscious. Darkness may also be associated with the *scotoma* in the eye—the point at which sensory impressions are not registered on the retina because of a knot of nerves leading to the brain, nerves which are absolutely necessary for any seeing at all to take place. Yet this knot of nerves produces the so-called blind spot: a darkness that is paradoxically the precondition of vision.

Finally, darkness can be associated with the unconscious, that unknowable repository of memory and fantasy—and, Wojnarowicz indicates, of collage. This collage component means that the millions of images "taken" by the eye are always being arranged and rearranged by the mind's eye. There is neither memory nor vision that is free of this subvision, that is "authentic," "real," or "true." Yet this limitation gives us a kind of freedom. "To remember perfectly would be forever to inhabit the same cultural order," Kaja Silverman writes. She goes on to argue that imperfect memory, memory that never quite arrives at its destination, gives us the opportunity to reread the world in new terms. When our imperfect memory "forgets," this is not necessarily a bad thing: we may be forgetting something we never had in the first place, something preinvented for us by established ways of seeing. Forgetting, she concludes, represents "the possibility of apprehending the world under conditions other than those dictated in advance by the given-to-be-seen."[18]

Much of what Silverman says here can be applied to Wojnarowicz's attack on the preinvented world, an attack that takes place in darkness, and through darkness. We recall that forgetting is for Freud one of the surest signs of a rift in the constructed wholeness of the subject. It leads into the dark unconscious, which is swarming with images. Yet these images are not an end in themselves; indeed they cannot possibly reach such an end. In Wojnarowicz's work we have a state like that described by Maurice Blanchot, "where the image, instead of alluding to some particular feature, becomes an allusion to the featureless, and instead of a form drawn upon absence, becomes the formless presence of this absence, the opaque, empty opening onto that which is when there is no more world, when there is no world yet."[19] Wojnarowicz's work plays modes of representation against one another to the point that "there is no more world," if by "world" we mean a stable and unanimous vision. At the same time this dissolution opens a way into possibility: in the absence of the preinvented world, "there is no world yet" and politics can literally visualize a new one. It is for this reason, and not some facile nihilism, that Wojnarowicz writes "I am crawling around looking for the aperture of complete and final emptiness."[20] In seeking to crawl *into* the dark room of the camera, Wojnarowicz is not necessarily turning away from his life and his world. For turning, as he has said, is "the moment that disrupts the vision." It is the moment both of disappearance and appearance, of losing the form in darkness and finding it. To turn into the darkness of subvision is to enter the place where vision has always been made and can always be made again.

The Color of the Mind's Eye

"I wish I could get a selective lobotomy and rearrange my senses so that all I could see is the color blue; no images or forms, no sounds or sensations."[21] The best gloss on this peculiar statement by Wojnarowicz is Derek Jarman's film *Blue*, which it uncannily anticipates. *Blue* was Jarman's last film, directed while he was going blind as a result of AIDS. What the film audience sees is easily described. At first the screen is a rectangle of raw white light; it would seem to be a projectionist's error were it not for the voice narrating, describing, chanting, musing. After a few minutes the screen switches abruptly to blue and remains so for the rest of the film. Seeing only what Jarman is able to see, we experience his descent into blindness and illness: the repeated visits to the hospital, the memories of friends already claimed by the disease, the attempts to come to terms with what is happening. It is a sadly familiar and nevertheless unassimilable story; the featureless screen reflects our blank incomprehension. Yet by the end of the film, something has come out of this nothing. Out of the narrator's words images have been born, images in the mind's eye. And that imaging process ultimately implies not an easy escapism but a politics of vision. This explains why a film that is explicitly and movingly about AIDS devotes much of its time to meditations on vision, both physical and psychical, and on the multifoliate significance of a single color, blue.

Blue is, in many senses, an afterimage. To begin with, the white light at the film's opening can be identified with a certain diagnostic procedure: "The shattering bright light of the eye specialist's camera leaves the empty sky-blue after-image."[22] But whereas in reality "the after-image dissolves in a second," Jarman's film slows down that afterimage, moves into it and muses on all that is consequent to the blinding revelation of his diagnosis. Listening, we soon realize that in a curious way he almost welcomes the loss of images. As Jarman's state becomes one that could indeed be ironically described as "after image," he asserts that he is also *anti*-image. "From the bottom of your heart, pray to be released from image," he says. This is because "the image is a prison of the soul" (115). But this all-blue film, which seems to blind the filmgoer's eye, opens the prison door:

> In the pandemonium of image
> I present you with the universal Blue
> Blue an open door to soul
> An infinite possibility
> Becoming tangible. (112)

In what sense, we must then ask, is blue "an open door to soul"?

One answer is provided by Kandinsky in his book *Concerning the Spiritual in Art*. In contrast to an active, forthcoming color like yellow, Kandinsky says, blue "moves into itself, like a snail retreating into its shell, and draws away from the spectator."[23] But not without drawing the spectator with it, for the eye is "absorbed" into blue. Citing Kandinsky, William Gass reiterates these ideas in his own "philosophical inquiry," *On Being Blue*: "Because blue contracts, retreats, it is the color of transcendence, leading us away in pursuit of the infinite."[24] "It is therefore most suitable as the color of interior life" (75–76)—but an interior life, Jarman would stress, that leads us away from exterior image to a simultaneous loss of sight and gain of visionary insight. "Blue drags black with it," he says, and "Blue is darkness made visible."[25] "Darkness made visible," of course, echoes Milton's famous paradox; it also underscores the fundamental paradox of the film: the fact that despite the claims for an escape from image, for attaining a state that is after image, image returns in visionary form.

The first return of image occurs as the viewer sees, or seems to see, irregularities in the blue projected field. Surely this is not *just* a flat field of color: are there not subtle shadowy forms behind the blue scrim? This kind of imagery is not uncommon under conditions of visual deficiency, conditions that fall into three classes:

1. *Absence of light*. Darkness or closed eyes may induce the imagery of hypnagogia or waking dreams.

2. *Homogenous visual fields*. Undifferentiated fields such as fog or blue sky are given differentiation by the eye, which projects images.

3. *Randomized visual fields*. Cloud formations and starry skies, for instance, have commonly been read as images.[26]

Moviegoers staring at the blue screen experience the second of these conditions—the so-called Ganzfeld Effect. It is as if the mind cannot endure pure ground, but must play figures against it, if only those of its own erratic physical vision. So irregular movements of the eye produce a sense of irregularities in the perceived field, which are then interpreted by the mind's eye as images.

After a while, the viewer comes to the realization that in fact the blue screen is undifferentiated and will remain so. At this point a second return of the image occurs, less bound up with the physical eye and more with the mind's eye, or the imagination: I am speaking of the visions that are generated by words. If blue is "an open door to soul," it is also, according to Gass, "the color of the mind . . . it is the color consciousness becomes when caressed; it is the dark inside of sentences, sentences which follow their own turnings inward out of sight like the whorls of a shell" (57). This sentence itself has many rich turns. A phrase like "the dark inside of sentences" (sentences which we nevertheless see and read) evokes the paradoxes of "darkness made visible." The turnings that sentences take "inward out of sight like the whorls of a shell" evoke Kandinsky's "snail retreating into its shell." Also, there may be echoes of the way that Wordsworth, in book 5 of *The Prelude*, describes the effects of sentences:

> There, darkness makes abode, and all the host
>   Of shadowy things work endless changes.
>   (lines 598–99)

These changes are worked by "the turnings intricate of verse" (line 603) which, moving inward, generate insight in "flashes" of "light divine"—yet another version of darkness made visible.

Beyond all the devices of the movie's evocative sound track, it is the mystery of words that generates in the viewer of *Blue* a movie of the mind, a blue movie. Jarman's own choice of words at one point hints at this. Just before praying to be released from image, Jarman gives us the reason for this prayer: "Accustomed to believing in image, an absolute idea of value, his world had forgotten the command of essence: Thou Shalt Not Create Unto Thyself Any Graven Image, although you know *the task is to fill the empty page*."[27] "Page," not screen or canvas. Of Jarman's multiple talents, he has selected writing to demonstrate the tyranny of the image. Yet at the same moment that he is reminding us "Thou Shalt Not" he is also saying "You Must"—must fill the empty page. This ambivalence of Jarman's toward image is best considered by viewing image from both its sides, always aware that these may be two sides of a *page*—that the image we are considering is in some way literary.

Image tyrannizes us, Jarman says, when it is viewed as an "absolute idea of value." He does not explain exactly what that absolute idea is. It probably ranges from the popular sense of "image" associated with the media, through the subtler conceptualization of image we find in a novel like Milan Kundera's *Immortality*, to the self-formative image of Lacan's mirror stage. The Lacanian model, especially, explains an extreme assertion like "The image is a prison of the soul, your heredity, your education, your vices and aspirations, your qualities, your psychological world" (115). In Lacan, selfhood in all of its aspects is thrust upon one through the image of self in the mirror, an image that all too rapidly becomes assimilated into the symbolic system, which is associated above all with language. Because language is an unstable system, where "meaning" slides from one signifier to another, any self who hopes to recapture the delusory wholeness of that first mirror image is doomed to lose selfhood in the very act of pursuing it; the signifying chain leads only to the manacled self.

But there is another side to image, asserted by Jarman in *Blue* precisely through an extended verbal image, one with many allusive layers.

"The dog barks, the caravan passes," this section begins; and then: "Marco Polo stumbles across the Blue Mountain" (113). The explorer seeks yet another strangely significant city, as he does in Italo Calvino's *Invisible Cities*. In that book all cities are perhaps only one city, and their various peculiarities are ways of reminding us of our modes of experiencing the lives that we build like cities around us. Most of all, Calvino may have structured his book to remind us of the visualization engendered by words, as has been argued by Ellen Esrock.[28] And Jarman may have intended something similar in providing a new city for discovery by both Marco Polo and the autobiographical narrator he has named Blue.

The city that Marco Polo seeks is called Aqua Vitae. Its name links it with alchemical processes, and especially with the element mercury: "Mercury was sovereign of the metals, it was both silver and red, it was the mirror and path to the Conjunctio. It was seen as the primordial water, guide and psychopomp" (76). So says Jarman in a section of his book *Chroma* entitled "Alchemical Colour." The fact that each stage of the alchemist's process was linked with a characteristic color indicates that Jarman's interest in color is ultimately an interest in transformative process. Here that transformative process is, among other things, that of words—as becomes clearer the further we progress in the description of the city.

First we encounter "mirror and path" combined: the road to the city of Aqua Vitae is protected by a labyrinth "built from crystals and mirrors which in the sunlight cause terrible blindness. The mirrors reflect each of your betrayals, magnify them and drive you into madness" (113). The "terrible blindness" here is initially that produced by the optometrist's mirror flash. But the mirrors also reflect the image of one's self, in a distorted version of Lacan's mirror stage. And the consequences of the mirror stage can indeed "drive you into madness," a madness that is the subject of Lacanian psychoanalysis.

Yet at the heart of this labyrinth, beyond the shattering of sight, is born a second sight, this time out of words:

Blue walks into the labyrinth. Absolute silence is demanded of all its visitors, so their presence does not disturb the poets who are directing the excavations. . . .

The archaeology of sound has only just been perfected and the systematic cataloguing of words has until recently been undertaken in a haphazard way. Blue watched as a word or phrase materialized in scintillating sparks, a poetry of fire which cast everything into darkness with the brightness of its reflections. (113)

The excavated words are "scintillating sparks" (likely a reference to the volume entitled *Silex Scintillans* by the seventeenth-century hermetic poet Thomas Vaughan). They are a source of light—light that once again, paradoxically, produces darkness, "casts everything into darkness with the brightness of its reflections." These reflections are both like and unlike the reflections in the mirrors flanking the roadway. They are like them in the blindness they produce, the paradoxical birth of darkness out of excessive light. But they are unlike the mirror reflections in that there is no indication here of what is reflected. We can only be sure that it is not an image of self-betrayal, nor of self. Perhaps the word *reflections* should be read not so much optically as etymologically: a "bending back" upon itself is the reflexive source of the blinding light of words. This bending may be related to Wordsworth's "turnings intricate of verse" or Gass's "sentences which follow their own turnings inward out of sight like the whorls of a shell": a labyrinth of quite another kind.

The light of words here casts everything into darkness—but perhaps a darkness made visible, the darkness of the unconscious illuminated. Yves Bonnefoy has written an essay called "Lifting Our Eyes from the Page" in which he argues that the effect of poetry, when it is most itself, is to cause us to stop reading, to lift our eyes from the page and sense a power that is purely inconceivable. In a sense, our eyes are blinded by the power of words; even the words that have ignited this illuminatory moment can no longer be seen by the reader's eye. It may be this kind of blindness—the blindness of insight—that results from the brilliance of words.

All this is mystical, paradoxical; the same words and images—blindness, for instance—are used to describe both Jarman's idea of prison and his idea of release from it. Such contradictions extend to the very idea of image itself. At one point, Jarman prays to be released from image, and after doing so asks himself "For what are you seeking?" His answer is "The fathomless blue of Bliss"—which would seem to be imageless. Yet when bliss is attained, it is attained *as an image*. In speaking of "bliss in my ghostly eye," Jarman is recalling the image of a lover, probably a dead lover:

Dead good looking
In beauty's summer
His blue jeans
Around his ankles

The eye that envisions this bliss is "ghostly" in two senses. First, it is an immaterial eye as opposed to the material one. Second, it is an eye haunted by the insubstantial ghosts that are mental images, whether produced or reproduced. It is thus the mind's eye that allows the escape into bliss, and does so in this film before all else through the instrumentality of words.

That instrumentality works not only to produce images in the mind's eye but to produce change in the world—that is, the image-making capacity of words is political. Jarman's film is not just an aesthetic exploration of certain aspects of visualization. It is also, we must remember, a film about AIDS, a record of real losses, and a dramatic cry of protest. The aesthetic and the political aspects of the film are not such strange bedfellows as may at first appear. For in Jarman's distrust of the tyranny of image and his speculation about the way alternative interior images are created, we see both a rebellion and a hope.

Our strongest ally where hope is concerned is of course Ernst Bloch, whose magisterial three-volume work *The Principle of Hope* recovers this usually Christianized virtue for Marxism. Hope for Bloch is an anticipatory mode working in the world, founded in materiality but moving beyond the mere status quo: "This hope is not taken *only as emotion*, as the opposite of fear (because fear too can of course anticipate), but more essentially as a directing act of a cognitive kind (and here the opposite is then not fear, but memory)."[29] Hope is that which impels us into the future—but not a passive future, carried on the impersonal current of time; rather a future that is anticipated, that is, in fact, visualized. It is this directing act, when the material conditions are propitious, that causes the New to emerge in the world. Hope is thus neither lack nor fulfillment, but something that moves *between* these states. For Bloch, hope as process is more authentic and essential than any entity or idea that has been hypostatized in its finished form: "The Authentic or essence is that *which is not yet, which in the core of things drives towards itself, which awaits its genesis in the tendency-latency of process*" (1373). In the present moment, a moment that continually leans beyond itself toward that which is not yet present, the authentic manifests itself as the principle of hope.

In the world process that Bloch describes, art has a special function: "Art is a laboratory and also a feast of implemented possibilities, together with the thoroughly experienced alternatives therein" (216). "Pre-appearance" is the function of art, Bloch says—but we should not make the mistake of assuming that the important thing is that which appears. Rather it is the fact of preappearance itself that is important, manifesting the human capacity to shape out of the objective and real a *Novum*, something new. As we experience art, play in its laboratory of possibilities, we see beyond any *particular* vision what Bloch calls "the process-world, the real world of hope itself" (1374).

Perhaps, indeed, all seeing is infused with the principle of hope, which yearns beyond the present moment. That present moment is always, Bloch claims, a blind spot. We cannot know its meaning except in the context of a process which has still to be finished. If the lived moment, as moment, is always dark, that darkness is nevertheless restless, it "ferments," in Bloch's phrase; its Not becomes Not-yet, and thus a kind of anticipatory consciousness that takes us out of the dark moment.

Bloch's terms are strikingly literalized in Jarman's *Blue*. This film strikes its viewers blind—not only in the sense just spoken of, pertaining to the present moment, but in a more apocalyptic sense. In speaking of "aesthetically attempted pre-appearance," Bloch asks, "how could the world be perfected without this world being exploded and apocalyptically vanishing?" (215). Such an apocalyptic vanishing immediately confronts viewers of Jarman's film. But then, even while mourning the dead, while describing the sufferings of the living scourged by AIDS, description itself evokes appearance in the mind's eye. And this formative activity rescues the film from being merely a passion, in the sense of something suffered. Filmed images of AIDS would have entered the eye passively, and not necessarily with any sense of hope or the capacity for change. Images in the mind's eye, because they are actively created, remind us that darkness can stir into a gradual becoming; that interior images can shape themselves in ways that are subtler and more multileveled than exterior ones that claim to define us; that there is a power within us that links us to the "process-world," that which creates process in the world.

Thus when the film ends with the words "I place a delphinium, Blue, upon your grave," this is no mere funeral tribute. The color of the delphinium echoes the name given the protagonist; and both are associated with the color of visualization, more hopeful than the traditional green. The film *Blue* is, in a sense, that blue flower. While it does not deny death's finality, it speaks of the encounter with death in such a way that we must also be aware of a process that continues, always. That process is Bloch's principle of hope. Here it is represented by visualization, or the power of preappearance in the mind's eye; and that power, we are reminded, vividly infuses any transformative politics.

Holographesis

Bloch's version of hope is a recuperation for Marxism of the idea of utopia. Beginning with his first book, *The Spirit of Utopia*, Bloch conceived of utopia as something more than just a wishful daydream—though both the wish and the daydream are manifestations of a utopian impulse. This impulse can be harnessed in a militant and material process. So, Bloch says, "the utopian function is transcendent without transcendence. Its support and correlate is process, which has not yet surrendered to its most immanent What-content, but is still under way. Which consequently is itself a state of hope."[30] Bloch was lecturing at the University of Leipzig when Christa Wolf was a student there, and his ideas are echoed at intervals in her work.[31] An explicit utopianism is also found in the work of another feminist, the Quebecois lesbian writer Nicole Brossard. "In my Universe," Brossard has said, "Utopia would be a fiction from which would be born the generic body of the thinking woman."[32] Here the word *fiction*, I think, refers not so much to utopia's fabular or mythic status as to the making of novels: making a feminist fiction involves remaking the idea of woman. This is in keeping with Bloch's ideas on the utopian function of art. The writer's words can evoke a vision that lies beyond both words and the present moment. In capitals, Brossard declares: "J'EVOQUE. JE CERTIFIE MON ESPOIR" (150).

Brossard's version of hope is a markedly visual one; it is *l'espoir en hologramme*,[33] holographic hope. The hologram pervades her 1982 novel *Picture Theory*, is at the heart of its aesthetics and its politics.

A hologram is basically an interference pattern, the kind that is produced when stones are dropped into a pond and their expanding circles overlap; as in Coleridge's "The Picture," "a thousand circlets spread, / And each mis-shape[s] the other" (lines 93–94). The interference pattern of a hologram is produced by splitting a laser beam: one part is bounced off an object, the other part is bounced off a mirror. Both parts of the beam meet again on holographic film, where they form the interference pattern. When, later, a laser beam is projected through that patterned film, an image of the object appears that is three-dimensional and apparently suspended in space. One can walk around it and watch its contours shift just as one would with a physical object. Perhaps the most peculiar property of the hologram is that every part of the film contains the whole: the film can be cut into pieces and every piece will have the same ability to project the image.

This property struck the neurophysiologist Karl Pribram with the force of a revelation when in the mid-1960's he read an article on holograms in *Scientific American*. He saw a startling similarity to a property of the brain: that even when large portions of the brain are removed, a person's memories are retained. In contradiction to earlier experiments that seemed to indicate that specific memories were associated with specific parts of the brain, it now appeared that each part of the brain contained the whole of memory. The same thing was true for vision: in experiments it was found that huge portions of the visual cortex could be excised (up to 98 percent) without affecting the ability of laboratory animals to do tasks requiring complex visual skills. Pribram began to hypothesize that the brain's functioning was holographic. At this point, he turned to physics and discovered the work of David Bohm, who had been led to the conviction that not just the brain but the entire universe functioned according to holographic principles. A colleague of Einstein at Princeton and a respected authority on quantum physics, Bohm was led past the quantum to the idea of frequencies. A universe of overlapping frequencies would create interference patterns similar to those of the hologram, in this way unfolding the phenomena of the physical world. The dualism of material and immaterial is dissolved; consciousness is on the same continuum as physical matter. This theory explained certain troubling behaviors of quanta; it also, logically, abolished time and space as fundamental categories. The result is a universe not unlike that which William Blake maintained against Newton. Bohm's physics offers a way of explaining all kinds of paranormal phenomena which the current paradigm of science relegates to the realm of the "nonscientific" and superstitious.[34]

Theories such as these would appeal to a writer like Brossard because of the power they give to thought, a power for far-reaching, fundamental change. As Michael Talbot has put it, "in a holographic universe, a universe in which separateness ceases to exist and the innermost processes of the psyche can spill over and become as much a part of the objective landscape as the flowers and the trees, reality itself becomes little more than a mass shared dream" (285). *Pour écrire, rêver est un accessoire*, Brossard writes: dreaming is an accessory to writing.[35] And, one may add, to reading. The reading of Brossard's text, of any text, is an act of consciousness which changes that consciousness in the process. To change consciousness, in a holographic universe, is to change reality, to unfold in certain directions what Bohm would call the implicit universe. So when Brossard refers to "the thinking woman" in the passage I first quoted, this is not some vague praise, as in "the thinking woman's cigarette"; a woman's thinking is a power that can unfold her into fully dimensioned reality. And this dimensioned reality may be projected out of the flat "film" of the page in an act of utopian vision.

Picture Theory, Brossard has entitled her novel, using the English words even in the original French version. The words are famously associated with Ludwig Wittgenstein's ultimately discarded idea, quoted in Brossard's text, that "A proposition is a picture of reality." Brossard's novel reverses the direction of this sentence, in which language and image are passively dependent on reality. In Brossard's holographic version, language generates image generates reality. But how exactly is this to be done?

"Studious girls, we will divert the course of fiction, dragging with us words turn and turn about, igneous spiral, picture theory an existence in these terms."[36] The idea of writing in a spiral is, for Brossard, the most effective strategy for women enclosed in the circle of a language that does not speak them. Breaking through the circle directly, if it could be done, would get women nothing but the silence and incoherence that has traditionally been their portion. It is far more effective to follow the contours of language, with a difference. Circling language at its outer edges, the woman writer uses words tangentially, at a tangent to their usual meanings while still touching those meanings: "I was tempted one day to conquer reality, to make it plausible. First by insinuation, slipping a few words in slantwise" (77). Repeated tangents create another circle, one that is almost congruent to the one initially given, but is independent of it, lifting away, turn and turn about spiraling outward. The given circle is not broken, then—a futile endeavor—but is opened up, unfolded out of the implicit.

The role of the picture in this theory is not inconsequential. Among many quotations from Djuna Barnes's *Nightwood* incorporated in Brossard's novel is this one: "An image is a stop the mind makes between uncertainties" (25). The uncertainties here are those of words, those created by Brossard's use of words. Words of course never mean "exactly" what they say, despite the force of conventional agreement. A deliberately slant-wise use of words brings to the fore the uncertainties inherent in language—as Lacan would put it, the incessant sliding of the signified under the signifier. In effect, an interference pattern is created between a word's conventional associations and the present unconventional use of it. The ripple effect of interference patterns as they are seen on holographic film has an equivalent as well in the fact that Brossard's "slantwise" words recur throughout the text, expanding into patterns of repetition. When the same phrase occurs in varying contexts this puts, as it were, a different slant on it; a phrase's initial tangential use creates an uncertainty which is rendered more uncertain as the phrase is repeated. But this uncertainty is only in regard to conventional ways of reading. At some point, the interference patterns create not uncertainty but resolution. One reads in the space *between*, as in Irigaray, and projects there an image resolved out of the force field of the text. Reading takes place in the space of a virtual reality whose end product, at the novel's end, is the image of virtual woman. This is Brossard's "indispensable trajectory: to unfold the real itself the space activated by holographic material" (128). And it is her re-vision of Wittgenstein's picture theory.

Brossard's novel describes the love between the narrator and Claire Dérive, whose name has certain holographic implications. *Dérive* means "leeway," the tendency of a ship to drift off course toward the lee side, the one sheltered from the wind. Beginning with this nautical definition, a host of related terms unfold: *à la dérive* refers figuratively to a deviation from course, any course of action; *dériver* is to divert (attention, the course of a river); and there are of course the senses in which one speaks of a word's derivation or that of a mathematical function. This cluster is in itself an example of language's tendency to drift. That passive drift becomes active deviation in Brossard's writing—which is used in the service of another "deviation" from the assigned course, that of the lesbian.

Brossard's *dérive* reverses the direction of Derrida's *différance* in that she uses the instability of language not to deconstruct claims of wholeness and coherence within the text, but to construct a virtual wholeness for woman that through the text is projected outside of it. The distinction between what is "inside" a structure and what is "outside" it was of course put into question by Derrida in his pivotal essay "Structure, Sign, and Play in the Discourse of the Human Sciences." He did this by exploring the paradoxes involved in the idea of a center, whose function it is to "orient, balance and organize the structure."[37] The most logical structure to be balanced and organized around a center is the circle, the very emblem of wholeness. This seems to be the icon that lies behind Derrida's essay, as the spiral lies behind Brossard's novel. But arguments based on the circle must be revised in the case of the spiral. Because its line is open, the spiral is subject to no clear distinction between "inside" and "outside." Yet we are not in a situation of free play either, for centripetal force curves the spiral's line into an accord with what has come before, even while centrifugal force ensures that the line will never meet in closure, will increasingly open up. It is a process that is somewhat like the derivation of a variable in calculus, in that it will never reach its limit point—and we should recall that it was Jean Fourier's version of the calculus that was used to invent the hologram in the first place.

Claire Dérive's first name, with its evocation of clarity and light, reminds us that interference patterns are not in themselves enough to produce a virtual image: a laser beam is necessary. In *Picture Theory* the laser's light is represented by "the white scene," an intense encounter between Claire and the narrator. Like so much else in the novel, this element is returned to repeatedly. But it is undoubtedly significant, in the light of the holographic mechanics that create interference patterns on film, that the whiteness of the laser beam is split so that "there are two scenes. One dated the 16th of May, the other very close to it. The book scene and the rug scene" (23). Both scenes culminate in lovemaking, whose white-hot intensity *is* the laser. The bodies of the lovers are shot through with light, are the equivalent of holographic film: "Conjugated with the lighting, the pleasure of audacity dangerously clothes the body of the other with an existential film from which arises, condensed in an image, the harmony that makes sense"[38] (the idea of making sense here punningly incorporates the kind of manifestation that is produced through a patterning of frequencies). Sections of the book are entitled "Screen Skin," "Screen Skin Too," "Screen Skin Utopia." This bodily screen is again holographic film, as well as an implied critique of the concept of "screen" found in Lacan. The screen is graphed by Lacan as midway between the gaze and the apparent spatial location of the picture; it "forms the mediation from the one to the other

[and] operates, not because it can be traversed, but on the contrary because it is opaque."[39] This opacity has led Kaja Silverman to identify the screen as "the site at which the gaze is defined for a particular society."[40]

In contrast to both these assertions, the screen for Brossard is traversable; it offers "the extravagance of surfaces, transparence of the holographed scene" (23). Remembering that *extravagance* etymologically means "straying outside," we see that this version of the screen does not function as the opaque site of an already defined vision. The effects of the holographic version are less predictable than that. They depend on patterns of traversal determined by two overlapping frequencies. These overlapping frequencies, in Brossard's multivalent metaphor, may arise from two sexual encounters or the two participants in those encounters; they may arise from two readings of a word, one conventional and the other "slantwise"; they may arise from the encounter between reader and author, never in perfect accord, at the surface of the page. In all these versions, the screen is not the opaque adjunct to a semblance of seeing, a seeing predefined by social expectations. Rather, the screen is part of an unpredictable process by which a new vision itself can come into being.

In the Lacanian production of "self," the mirror initiates the split subject into a process of unceasing alienation. In the mechanics of hologram production the mirror's role is to transmit the split beam of the laser, which returns to itself, never in perfect congruence, but in such a way that the discrepancies or interferences produce a resolution beyond themselves. Brossard contra Lacan asserts the possibilities of a mirroring that is more than a series of deferrals of the already determined. The argument is made by metaphor, utilizing image to argue for the power of image. This image is also an ideology, in Althusser's redefinition of the term within the Lacanian system: ideology is "the 'representation' of the Imaginary relationship of individuals to their Real conditions of existence."[41] In regard to this definition, Fredric Jameson comments, "Ideological representation must . . . be seen as that indispensable mapping fantasy or narrative by which the individual subject invents a 'lived' relationship with collective systems which otherwise by definition exclude him insofar as he or she is born into a pre-existent social form and its pre-existent language."[42] The word "otherwise" here offers a hope for change which is perhaps balanced by the word "lived," in quotation marks. Brossard's holographic ideology provides neither last word nor final image, only a calculated strategy. Calculus-like, it approaches a final limit that it can never attain completely. But that projected approach is, if not wholeness and presence, a force for change, a way to reinvent the preinvented world: "At the end of patriarchal night the body anticipates on the horizon I have in front of me on the screen of skin, mine, whose resonance endures in what weaves the text/ure t/issue *the light*."[43]

"Travaille ta braise en hologramme," Brossard writes; and then in italics "*c'est solution des yeux*." Barbara Godard translates this accurately as "Work your embers into a hologram, *it's the eyes' solution*."[44] However, some of the higher frequencies are necessarily lost in translation. Embers and eyes are connected in the French phrase *des yeux de braise*, meaning "ardent." Embers must now be kindled beyond the conventional fires of passion into white laser light. Such a light is not merely a tool for seeing, an adjunct to seeing; it is the means of literally projecting a new visual reality. And, it may be, a new concept of seeing. For if a utopian vision is in some sense "the eyes' solution" to the political dilemma of the lesbian, it is a solution that comes at some cost to the eyes themselves. *Solution des yeux* can mean not only the solution provided by the eyes, but the *dis*solution of the eyes. Indeed, one involves the other. We have seen how seeing, in Wojnarowicz, must strike itself blind if it is to get past the vision of the preinvented world. We have seen in Jarman how, out of blindness, a second sight is born of the visualization engendered by words. And in Brossard we see how words can project a fully dimensioned image into the world, a world that in this way can begin to be reinvented.

Afterimage

All books must end, and no book ever does. Physically, of course, the covers are closed and the book put away, but inside the covers is a constellation of elements capable of almost infinite variations. Consequently, the work of interpretation, like the proverbial women's work, is never done. Books come to be seen anew through juxtaposition with other books; they may even generate new books, like Prospero's promiscuous library. Indeed, since no book ever stands sole and single, but intertextually incorporates many other books, every book is already a library. One last book will be added to this book's library. Michael Ende's *The Neverending Story* is something of an international phenomenon—a children's book that because of its complex metaphysical patterning was taken seriously by adults. As its title indicates, it is a book about the impossibility of ending, a Möbius strip of a book whose crucial twist is visualization.

The Neverending Story is the story of a boy who enters a book. Unhappy, neglected by his grief-stricken father since his mother's death, chubby and graceless, Bastian Balthazar Bux takes refuge from the teasing of other children in an old bookstore. While there he is impelled to steal a wondrous-looking book entitled *The Neverending Story*. Hiding in the attic of his school, he gradually becomes absorbed by the book—and then, suddenly and literally, he is absorbed *into* it—into the fictional kingdom, kingdom of fiction, Fantastica. Here he can be transformed into a Bastian of the kind he has always wanted to be: handsome, athletic, resourceful, brave. He is now a hero, displacing the book's previous hero. But what is then played out is a critique of the very idea of heroism.[1] Bastian's manly virtues become perverted—or rather are shown to be innately perverse—leading to the near ruin of Fantastica and of himself. Turning away from control, power, and self-aggrandizement, Bastian wanders through Fantastica lost and confused. All he can do is to follow the directive engraved on the magic gem Auryn, given to him as a talisman: "Do What You Wish." This does not mean that one is to do anything one feels like, Bastian is told: "It means that you must do what you really and truly want. And nothing is more difficult."[2] Whenever such a wish is fulfilled, Bastian must pay the usual price, which is the loss of one of his memories.

When he has forgotten all of his past except his own name, Bastian comes, in the book's penultimate chapter, to the picture mine of Yor. The miner Yor is an old man, stone gray and blind. "As he stood there motionless, he seemed carved from congealed lava. Only his blind eyes were dark, and deep within them there was a glow, as of a small, bright flame" (353). But, as he explains, "I am blind only in daylight. In the darkness of my mine, I can see" (353). No doubt this is because of the curious nature of the picture mine, which Yor describes in terms that evoke the unconscious: "Once someone dreams a dream, it can't just drop out of existence. But if the dreamer can't remember it, what becomes of it? It lives on in Fantastica, deep under our earth. There the forgotten dreams are stored in many layers. The deeper one digs, the closer together they are. All Fantastica rests on a foundation of forgotten dreams" (355). The dream images are described as being like fragile sheets of isinglass; these are detached from the mine and brought into the light of day, where they are spread out against the snow. Some of them are described:

There were figures in weird disguise that seemed to be flying through the air in an enormous bird's nest, donkeys in judge's robes, clocks as limp as soft butter, dressmaker's dummies standing in deserted, glaringly lighted squares. There were faces and heads pieced together from animals and others that made up a landscape. But there were also perfectly normal pictures, men mowing a wheat field, women sitting on a balcony, mountain villages and seascapes, battle scenes and circus scenes, streets and rooms and many, many faces, old and young, wise and simple, fools and kings, cheerful and gloomy. There were gruesome pictures, executions and death dances, and there were comical ones, such as a group of young ladies riding a walrus or a nose walking about and being greeted by passersby. (354)

We recognize images from Goya, Daumier, Dali, De Chirico, Arcimboldo, and the anamorphic tradition; a later excavation produces a group of images by Magritte. Images by painters are mingled with those generated by fiction (Gogol's "The Nose"). Day by day, Bastian descends into the darkness of the mine. Unable to see within that darkness, as Yor can, he has to work by feel. Every evening he brings images to the surface, spreads them out upon the whiteness, and searches them for something he does not know and cannot find. Then one day he brings up the picture of a man encased in a block of ice. It is the image of his father's plight, though Bastian no longer remembers his father. Nevertheless it moves him deeply, and provides the impetus for him to leave the mine and ultimately the realm of Fantastica.

Outside the book, once again fat and graceless, Bastian finds that he has not lost all of what he acquired within it: despite appearances, he is different, and it is clear that his relationship with his father will be different from now on. What he has lost, though, is the actual book; when he goes to confess this to the bookshop's owner he learns that such a book was never part of the shop's stock, but also that "every real story is a Neverending Story" (376). That this is so has already been indicated by the pictures of the mine, which are both described as forgotten dreams and recognized as works of art. One turns into the other, and the turn goes both ways. If Freud is right in asserting that the unconscious makes no distinction between reality and an "emotionally charged fiction," his assertion may apply not only to our own fantasies but, as well, to the fictions of others into which we enter imaginatively. Such an unconscious would not just be structured as a language, but as a fiction, as uncountable overlapping fictions. Dream images, after all, are both the foundation of Fantastica and its product. Image generates the author's text, which generates the reader's image—which generates an afterimage whose effects are unpredictable. They may contribute to the construction of a self, or of a politics, or to still more versions of Fantastica. Whatever its effects, the image remains, capable of other effects at other times. Compacted with other, consequent images, it lies forgotten in darkness—in Kant's phrase, an art hidden in the depths of the soul. There is no ending for the image but, happily or not, the traditional "ever after."

REFERENCE MATTER

Notes

ENTERING THE BOOK

1. Nabokov, *Lectures on Literature*, 4. This kind of observation is not an anomaly. Nabokov must have driven at least some of his students round the bend when his examination questions asked them to describe such things as Emma Bovary's hairdo.

2. Mitchell, chapter 1.

3. Bal, 135.

4. Blanchot, "Reading," 95.

5. Austen, letter to her sister Cassandra, May 24, 1813, *Letters*, 309–10.

6. "Jane Austen," in Woolf, *Collected Essays*, 1: 148.

7. Hemingway, 75.

8. Scarry, 20.

9. Rapaport, 17.

10. Freud, letter to Wilhelm Fliess, September 21, 1897, in *The Origins of Psychoanalysis*, 216.

11. Foucault, "Fantasia of the Library," in *Language, Counter-Memory, Practice*, 90. Actually Foucault argues that Flaubert's book marks the *beginning* of such literary phantasmagoria, ignoring many earlier works—for instance, Chaucer's *Book of the Duchess*—in which books are clearly seen to produce visionary experiences.

12. Bakhtin, 32.

CHAPTER 1: POSSESSED BY WORDS

1. Handke, *Absence*, 53.

2. Poulet, 58.

3. Gadamer, 111.

4. Kilgour, 139.

5. Jacobi, 286.

6. Cortázar, 63.

7. Castle, "Phantasmagoria," 56.

8. Collins, *Reading the Written Image*, xi.

9. Castle, "Spectralization," 248. Both of the essays by Castle that I have cited were later incorporated into her book *The Female Thermometer*.

10. First appearing in "Groundless Figures," Collins's theory was later incorporated into *The Poetics of the Mind's Eye*. Here I have used Collins's most recent formulation, "Writing and the Nature of the Supernatural Image."

11. Collins, "Writing and the Nature of the Supernatural Image," 251.

12. Scarry, 13.

13. Todorov, 25.

14. Freud, "The Uncanny," 226; emphasis mine.

15. Freud, "The Uncanny," 244. Cf. Paul de Man's comment "To make the invisible visible is uncanny," in *The Resistance to Theory*, 49.

16. The story is L. G. Moberly's "Inexplicable."

17. Celati, 80.

18. Cixous, 542–43.

19. Banville, *Ghosts*, 191. For an insightful analysis of how Charles Dickens is, in several senses of the phrase, a ghost writer, see A. H. Miller's article.

20. Compare the "little round" of the visual field as described by Collins:

> Our visual field is an oval lying on its side, outlined by our brows, cheekbones, and nose. It roughly measures 180 degrees in the horizontal projection and 150 degrees in the vertical. . . . As we become aware of this oval window of light, however, we discover that it is not uniformly clear. In fact, all but a tiny area is blurred. That tiny area, only about the size of our thumbnail held at arm's length, represents that segment of the visual array that the lens of each eye projects onto the *macula*, a mass of color-sensitive cone cells at the back of each retina within which lies the thickly packed *fovea*, used for minute examination of objects. (*The Poetics of the Mind's Eye*, 96)

21. Ortega y Gasset, 97: "Instead of defining his figures and their sentiments, the novelist must . . . evoke them in order that their self-presence may intercept our vision of the real world around us. Now, as far as I can see, there is no other way of achieving this but by supplying a wealth of detail. The reader must be caught in a dense web of innumerable minutely told circumstances."

22. Derrida, *Memoires for Paul de Man*, 34.

23. Defoe, viii.

24. Handke, *Across*, 130.

CHAPTER 2: DREAM BOOK

1. Banville, interview.

2. Blanchot, "Dreaming, Writing," xxii.

3. Gardner, *On Moral Fiction*, 179.

4. Gardner, *The Art of Fiction*, 30–31.

5. Freud, *The Interpretation of Dreams*, 525.

6. Lacan, "The Agency of the Letter," 147.

7. Grinstein, 66.

8. Grosz, 110.

9. Wordsworth, *The Prelude*, book 5, 122–26.

10. Freud, *Introductory Lectures on Psycho-analysis*, 180–81.

11. The project of botanical classification itself, according to Michel Foucault in *The Order of Things*, raises similar problems of representation. Here, too, visibility passes into discourse. It does so by way of *structure*, seen as intimately related to language.

> By means of structure, what [visual] representation provides in a confused and simultaneous form is analysed and thereby rendered suitable to the linear unwinding of language. . . . Whereas one and the same representation can give rise to a considerable number of propositions [compare Derrida's multiple readings of the image on the Bodleian library postcard], since the names that embody it articulate it according to different modes, one and the same animal, or one and the same plant, will be described in the same way, in so far as their structure governs their passage from representation into language. (136)

A comparable displacement of the visual into the linguistic occurs in Freud's systematization of dreams. Yet individual dreams resist this systematization, ultimately situating themselves within a rhizomic unconscious rather than "the linear unwinding of language." Considerations such as these lead Samuel Weber to declare in *The Legend of Freud* that "the dream works in and through a medium that is structurally irreducible to the predicative grammar of conscious thought" (67).

12. Lacan, "Of Structure as an Inmixing of Otherness," 187.

13. Ibid., 188.

14. Ellie Ragland-Sullivan's caution should be kept in mind here: "One common misreading of Lacan tends to link his Symbolic *je* to signifiers and speech, contrasting these with the Imaginary *moi*, images, and the visual and dividing these along conscious/unconscious lines. Lacan taught that the unconscious signifier is both image and sound but that the visual component has no meaning apart from the external language which names it." *Jacques Lacan and the Philosophy of Psychoanalysis*, 168–69.

15. Ragland-Sullivan, "The Magnetism Between Reader and Text," 404.

16. Ragland-Sullivan, *Jacques Lacan and the Philosophy of Psychoanalysis*, 235.

17. Lacan, *The Four Fundamental Concepts of Psycho-analysis*, 75.

18. Ragland-Sullivan, "The Magnetism Between Reader and Text," 386.

19. Mavromatis, 5, 14.

20. Nabokov, *Speak, Memory*, 34.

21. Nabokov, *Strong Opinions*, 47.

22. Woolf, *The Moment and Other Essays*, 109–10.

23. Koestler, 167.

24. Poulet, 58.

25. Blanchot, *The Space of Literature*, 32.

26. Ibid., 33.

27. One of the section headings of Victor Nell's *Lost in a Book* is the blunt statement "Reading Is Not Dreaming." The rationale for this statement is given in the chapter's fearlessly tautological epigraph, from Klinger: "Psychologically, when different states feel different, they are different." This is only good sense. Yet Nell is willing to admit that "the passivity of the reader's experience . . . closely resembles the passivity of the hypnagogic state" (208). Generally, Nell's discussion of the issue is marked by ambivalence and at times contradiction. Nor does he distinguish sufficiently between liminal imagery evolving at the edges of a reader's unconscious, and the effortful imaging used to solve problems such as "Is a horse's knee or the tip of its tail higher off the ground?"—to which I can't help observing that it depends on the length of the tail.

28. Wolf, *Cassandra*, 185.

29. Wolf, *What Remains and Other Stories*, 39. In his essay "'These Drowsy Approaches of Sleep,'" Andrew Winnard has demonstrated the prevalence of hypnagogic states in Wolf's work.

30. Wolf, *What Remains*, 43.

31. Wolf, *Cassandra*, 142.

32. Wolf, *The Author's Dimension*, 11.

33. Wolf, *Cassandra*, 161. Cf. Ionesco, 61: "Words have killed images or concealed them. A civilization based on words is a lost civilization."

34. Wolf, 151.

CHAPTER 3: SEEING THE FOREST FOR THE TREES

1. Ragland-Sullivan, *Jacques Lacan and the Philosophy of Psychoanalysis*, 29.

2. Paivio, 16.

3. Eco, 6.

4. Calvino, *The Baron in the Trees*, 217.

5. For a consideration of fiction under the aspect of embroidery, see J. Hillis Miller's essay "The Figure in the Carpet," which is also concerned with emptiness and fictional filling.

6. Irigaray, 137–38.

7. Ingarden, 52–53.

8. I would like to thank Michael Bishop of Dalhousie University's French department for clarifying the nature of the *blanc-seing*.

9. Foucault, *This Is Not a Pipe*, 24–25.

10. Iser, *The Act of Reading*, 178.

11. Gass, *Fiction and the Figures of Life*, 17.

12. Marr, *Vision*, 354.

13. Ashbery, 90. I owe this reference to Elaine Scarry.

14. For a readable summary of Kosslyn's theories at the time, see his *Ghosts in the Mind's Machine*.

15. For his *Inquiries into Human Faculty and Its Development* (1883), Sir Francis Galton sent out a questionnaire to a hundred prominent men, asking them to recall the look of their breakfast table that morning, and then to report on the vividness of the image that came to them. The most striking result was the great range of vividness experienced. Examples at the extreme of this range are the famous case of S. V. Shereshevskii, whose tendency to translate *everything* into imagery allowed him to perform prodigious feats of memory; and, in contrast, a man designated as "R" who appears to have no mental imagery whatsoever. The case of "R" is reported by Robert Sommer in *The Mind's Eye*, 107–18; a brief account of Shereshevskii can be found in Hunter, 205–12.

16. Calvino, *If on a Winter's Night a Traveller*, 10.

17. Scarry, 12. Scarry is referencing Gibson, 215.

18. Calvino, *If on a Winter's Night a Traveller*, 11.

19. Sorrentino, 152.

20. Iser, "The Reading Process," 144–45.

21. Woolf, *To the Lighthouse*, 73.

22. See the chapter entitled "Linguistic Function and Literary Style," in Halliday, 103–40.

23. Bloch, *Essays on the Philosophy of Music*, 1.

24. Bloch, *The Principle of Hope*, 306.

CHAPTER 4: PAINTERS OF READING

1. Merleau-Ponty, "Eye and Mind," 175.

2. Kosslyn, 1–28.

3. Merleau-Ponty, *The Visible and the Invisible*, 248. The posthumous publication of *The Visible and the Invisible* is credited by Lacan with prompting his own thoughts on the gaze in *The Four Fundamental Concepts of Psycho-Analysis*, thoughts which may be seen as a kind of dialogue with the invisible Merleau-Ponty.

4. It is perhaps significant that Derrida has increasingly used visions and ghosts as epistemological models. See his *Memoires for Paul de Man*, and *Specters of Marx*.

5. Merleau-Ponty, *The Visible and the Invisible*, 192.

6. Merleau-Ponty, "Eye and Mind," 171.

7. Pater, "Apollo in Picardy," 143.

8. Brontë, 528.

9. See the chapter on "Medical, Physiological, and Psychoanalytic Theory" in Flint, *The Woman Reader*.

10. See Flaxman, *Victorian Word-Painting*.

11. Byron, *Don Juan*, canto 6, stanza 109.

12. Nabokov, *Speak, Memory*, 35.

13. Nabokov, *Bend Sinister*, 76.

14. Rimbaud, 110. Translation of "Voyelles" by James Lawler.

15. B. F. Skinner also explained his synesthesia by the associations with a childhood alphabet book. See his *Particulars of My Life*, 297.

16. Collier, "Lire 'Voyelles.'"

17. Lawler, 51.

18. Ibid., 52–53.

19. Merleau-Ponty, "Eye and Mind," 167.

20. Blanchot, "The Essential Solitude," in *The Space of Literature*, 33.

21. Andrew J. McKenna argues for a parallel between the aims of Freud and Rimbaud: "Invisible to consciousness, language is visible in the unconscious and one can describe Freudian interpretation as an effort to make language uninvisible. This effort is in many ways closely akin to Rimbaud's project" (221). However, Rimbaud does not rest content with Freud's rebuses. His visible language, in "Voyelles" as elsewhere, is of the kind implied by his title *Illuminations*: not only is the letter material, but "the word is literally filled with images, letter by rubricked letter" (Ibid., 233).

22. Merleau-Ponty, "Eye and Mind," 180.

23. Derrida, "+ R (Into the Bargain)," in *The Truth in Painting*, 169.

24. Derrida, *Memoirs of the Blind*.

25. Valéry, 1194.

26. Once formed, however, a piece of writing can be translated as a whole into a formal visual equivalent. The animator Oskar Fischinger, for instance, when he was to deliver a sort of "book report" for his reading group, produced long scrolls of evolving abstract forms to correspond to the *déroulements* of *Twelfth Night* and Fritz von Unruh's *Der Platz*. The scroll for Unruh's play is reproduced in Moritz, 97.

27. Tisseron, 33.

28. On Tolstoy's visualization, see Seifried, "Gazing on Life's Page," especially Seifried's analysis of Anna Karenina's state of mind while reading.

29. Gandelman, 127. For further examples of the manuscript drawings of authors, see Martine Reid's edition of *Yale French Studies* 84 (1994) under the title of *Boundaries: Writing and Drawing*—an outstanding collection, including essays on the manuscripts of Stendhal, Proust, Valéry, and Artaud; see also *The Writer's Drawing Book*, ed. Kate Pullinger and Julian Rothenstein.

30. Thévoz, 211.

31. Foster, 7.

32. Phillips, *Works and Texts*, 259.

33. If this is indeed a freshly plowed field, another plowed field becomes relevant: that depicted by Holbein and referenced by Ruskin, analyzed by J. Hillis Miller in his *Illustration*, 88–96. Miller's point is that there is a parallel between the furrows gouged by the plow and those gouged by the engraver's tool. Following

Heidegger, he argues that there is a *Riss*, a taking away, inherent in any human construction. On this point compare Merleau-Ponty on the nature of the line: "It is a certain process of gouging within the in-itself, a certain constitutive emptiness" ("Eye and Mind," 184).

34. It is appropriate that *Prospero's Books* exists in two versions: the published film script and the film, which is somewhat different in its details from the script's initial conception. Greenaway's script, which itself generates images in its readers, is preceded by the director's internal images, and then used to generate the cinematic realization of those images. I move freely between the images of the script and those of the realized film.

35. Greenaway, 57.

36. Foucault, "Fantasia of the Library," 90.

37. Iser, *The Act of Reading*, 148.

38. Merleau-Ponty, "Eye and Mind," 184–85.

CHAPTER 5: FRAMING THE FANTASM

1. Greenaway, 12.

2. Scarry, 17–21.

3. Derrida, *The Truth in Painting*, 61.

4. Kant, 68.

5. Derrida, *The Truth in Painting*, 61.

6. Aristotle, *Rhetoric*, 211.

7. Quintilian, *Institutio Oratio* 8.3.62; cited by Galyon, 31.

8. Elinor Schaffer has argued that Coleridge's *Aids to Reflection* anticipated Derrida's ideas on the *parergon*. See her "Illusion and Imagination." For the peritext, see Genette, *Paratexts*.

9. Schneider, *Coleridge, Opium, and Kubla Khan*.

10. Cf. Olds, 179: "Hallucinations and simile share the important characteristic of framing, and so combining, unrelated forms into a new composite entity."

11. Out of context and prefaced to "Kubla Khan," the fact that "the pool becomes a mirror" implies that what it mirrors is the face of the poet, also depicted at the poem's end. The scene would then be a version of the Well of Narcissus. Agamben, in *Stanzas: Word and Phantasm in Western Culture*, has analyzed the Well of Narcissus in relation to the *duecento* poets' notions of love as fantasm (while tying this in to notions of the word as fantasm). Coleridge's poem, too, implies that love is fantasmatic, making it the beloved lady whose image is reflected in the surface of the pool. Of course that image never *really* appears, but is only imagined to do so by the narrator. Reflection in the mind creates an imagined reflection in water, the fantasm of a fantasm. Yet the image is introduced so strongly ("Behold!") and in such detail that we may well be unsure whether all this is actually taking place or not. When the negation comes ("Not to thee, / O wild and

desert stream! belongs this tale") it protests too much. The lover pursues his resolution to find in nature a retreat from love, but the landscape that follows is now
compulsively read in amorous terms.

The picture in the mind's eye is followed by another picture, discarded by the
beloved after having been sketched on a piece of birch bark, and found by the
lover. Again, it is introduced equivocally. The narrator has been describing a cottage; exclaiming "But what is this?" he continues, apparently, to describe the cottage for six lines before he answers his own question by revealing that we are now
looking at "a curious picture." Taking the picture with him, the lover pursues the
artist. What his reception may be we do not know; this poem about lack of resolution lacks a resolution. But in any case it is really not so much a narrative as "a
psychological curiosity." And a metaphysical one, for the poem exhibits links between a number of fantasms: love, the mental creation of images, and an actual
drawing. It continually challenges us to distinguish these from one another and
from reality. Many of these questions of fantasms and conditional existence are replayed in another key in "Kubla Khan."

12. Coleridge, *Collected Works*, 4: 1, 142.

13. See Perkins, "Romantic Reading as Revery."

14. Schneider, 91–105.   15. Darwin, 47- 48.

16. Kames, 1: 112.   17. Alison, 40.

18. Coleridge, *Biographia Literaria*, 2: 222.

19. Christensen, 74.

20. Coleridge, *Collected Works*, 5: 2, 266.

21. Bachelard, xxii. See also "From the Window of a Train," in Birkerts, *The Gutenberg Elegies*. In part 1 of this collection of essays, Birkerts eloquently describes many of the aspects of reading that concern me here.

22. Blake, 729.

23. John Gardner, *On Moral Fiction*, 202–3. Gardner's last novel, *Mickelson's Ghosts*, shuttles between ghosts as traditionally conceived and the fantasms of a
troubled mind, so that each becomes a version of the other.

24. In chapter 14 of the *Biographia Literaria*, Coleridge describes the "pleasur-
able activity of mind" excited in the reader: "Like the motion of a serpent, which
the Egyptians made the emblem of intellectual power . . . at every step he pauses
and half recedes, and from the retrogressive movement collects the force which
again carries him onward" (2: 11).

25. Derrida, *The Truth in Painting*, 32.

26. Pearce, 581.

27. Derrida, *The Truth in Painting*, 61.

28. Coleridge, *Notebooks*, 1: 1, entry 1765.

29. Derrida, "Living On / BORDER LINES," 90–91.

30. Derrida, *Memoirs of the Blind*, 37.

31. Ibid., 45. On the nature of "theme," see Wolfgang Iser, whose stress on the

theme's "lack," its quality of not-yet-having-become, has a certain rapprochement with the invisibility of the line that is meant to (re)produce it: "As the theme is not an end in itself, but a sign for something else, it produces an 'empty' reference, and the filling-in of this reference is what constitutes the significance. This is how ideation brings forth an imaginary object, which is a manifestation of that which was not formulated in the text." *The Act of Reading*, 147.

32. Coleridge, *Notebooks*, 1: 1, entry 1770.

33. Christensen, 268.

34. Compare the effect of full imaginative participation as described in Coleridge's poem "The Garden of Boccaccio":

> I see no longer! I myself am there,
> Sit on the ground-sward, and the banquet share.
>
> (lines 65–66)

35. Coleridge, *Notebooks*, 2: 1, entry 2583.

36. Derrida, *Memoirs of the Blind*, 68. In the light of the continuum being suggested here between inner vision and physical vision, it is worth noting the parallel continuum (more apparent in the eighteenth century) between the words *spectre* and *spectrum*. At their midpoint is the word *spectral*, which can refer either to fantoms or to the range of colors that make up light. *Spectrum*, indeed, can be used for both.

A Coleridge notebook entry that is pertinent to this and to much else in my argument is number 1681, written in November 1803. It begins, as "Kubla Khan" did, when Coleridge combines a quantity of laudanum with a book:

> Tho' I had 2 Candles near me, reading in my bed, I was obliged to magnify the Letters by bringing the Book close to my Eye—I then put out the Candles, & closed my eyes—& instantly there appeared a spectrum, of a Pheasant's Tail, that altered thro' various degradations into round wrinkly shapes, as of (Horse) Excrement, or baked Apples—indeed exactly like the latter—round baked Apples, with exactly the same colour, the same circular intra-circular Wrinkles—I started out of bed, lit my Candles, & noted it down, in order to state these circular irregularly concentric Wrinkles, something like Horse dung, still more like flat baked or (dried) Apples, such as they are brought in after Dinner.—*Why those Concentric Wrinkles?*

Coleridge then goes to the window "to empty my Urine-pot," and describes a night view, characterized first by what is *not* depicted in the "darkness & only not utter black undistinguishableness," and second by how much is nevertheless distinguished by the interpreting eye. At the close of this he breaks off to exclaim again "O that I could but explain these concentric Wrinkles in my Spectra!" Always willing to be helpful, I would suggest a connection between the "circular intra-circular Wrinkles" here and those on the surface of the stream in the preface to "Kubla Khan." These, as I have tried to argue, can be read in terms of the dynamics of the framing process. And it is that process which generates vision (the underlying preoccupation of the whole entry), whether it be the hypnagogic substratum made visible, or the shapes of the real world.

37. Heppner, "The Chamber of Prophecy."
38. Preston, 181–82.
39. Rosenblum, 190.
40. Heppner, "Blake as Humpty Dumpty," 232.
41. Clark, 166.

CHAPTER 6: A POLITICS OF VISUALIZATION

1. Phelan, 10. Thanks to Emily Givner for introducing me to Phelan's book.
2. Lacan, *Scilicet*, 120; cited in Phelan, *Unmarked*, 15. The capitalized "Other" refers to the Lacanian unconscious, or "internal other," in the quotation that follows; the small *o* "other" is Phelan's "external other," another person marked as different from oneself.
3. Phelan, *Unmarked*, 26.
4. *Aperture* 137 (Fall 1994): 2.
5. Wojnarowicz, *Memories That Smell Like Gasoline*, 47–48.
6. Wojnarowicz, *Close to the Knives*, 24–25.
7. Lippard, 21. Technically, Wojnarowicz may be experiencing not hypnagogic but *hypnapompic* imagery, the much rarer phenomenon of dream images persisting before the physical eye upon wakening.
8. Wojnarowicz, *Close to the Knives*, 26.
9. Silverman, 180.
10. Wojnarowicz, *Close to the Knives*, 26–27.
11. *Aperture*, 21.
12. Lippard, 7.
13. *Aperture*, 64.
14. Christian Metz, "Photography and Fetish," in Squiers, 158.
15. Blinderman, "Compression of Time," 56.
16. Wojnarowicz's text is taken from *Close to the Knives*, 62.
17. Wojnarowicz, *Close to the Knives*, 23.
18. Silverman, 189–90.
19. Blanchot, *The Space of Literature*, 33.
20. Lippard, 25.
21. Wojnarowicz, *Close to the Knives*, 114.
22. Jarman, 123. The section of this book entitled "Into the Blue" is, with only a couple of slight changes, the source of the film script of *Blue*, and is cited throughout this essay in preference to both the film/video and the CD (Elektra Nonesuch, 1994).
23. Kandinsky, 37.

24. Gass, *On Being Blue*, 76.

25. Jarman, 114.

26. I take these categories from Collins, *The Poetics of the Mind's Eye*, 156.

27. Jarman, 115; emphasis mine.

28. Esrock, 160–77.

29. Bloch, *The Principle of Hope*, 12.　30. Ibid., 146.

31. Kuhn, 8, 77–79, 149–53, 206.　　32. Brossard, 147.

33. Ibid., 168.

34. For a lucid and full study of the holographic paradigm, see Talbot, *The Holographic Universe*; also Wilber, *The Holographic Paradigm*.

35. Brossard, 21.

36. Ibid., 88.

37. Derrida, "Structure, Sign, and Play," 278.

38. Brossard, 27; translation modified.

39. Lacan, *The Four Fundamental Concepts of Psycho-Analysis*, 96.

40. Silverman, 135.

41. Althusser, "Ideology and Ideological State Apparatuses," 162.

42. Jameson, 394.

43. Brossard, 150.

44. Ibid., 83; page 94 in the original French edition.

AFTERIMAGE

1. See Leo Duroche's unpublished 1992 MLA paper "The Fragmented Self in Michael Ende's *Neverending Story*."

2. Ende, 201.

Works Cited

Agamben, Giorgio. *Stanzas: Word and Phantasm in Western Culture*. Minneapolis: University of Minnesota Press, 1993.

Alison, Archibald. *Essays on the Nature and Principles of Taste*. Hartford: G. Goodwin, 1821.

Althusser, Louis. "Ideology and Ideological State Apparatuses." In *Lenin and Philosophy, and Other Essays*, trans. Ben Brewster, 121–73. London: New Left Books, 1971.

Aristotle. *Rhetoric*. Trans. Lane Cooper. New York: Appleton-Century Crofts, 1932.

Ashbery, John. *As We Know*. New York: Viking, 1979.

Austen, Jane. *Jane Austen's Letters to her Sister Cassandra and Others*. Ed. R. W. Chapman. Oxford: Oxford University Press, 1979.

Bachelard, Gaston. *The Poetics of Space*. Trans. Maria Jolas. Boston: Beacon, 1964.

Bakhtin, Mikhail. *The Dialogic Imagination: Four Essays*. Austin: University of Texas Press, 1981.

Bal, Mieke. "Visual Poetics: Reading with the Other Art." In *Theory Between the Disciplines: Authority, Vision, Politics*, ed. Martin Kreiswirth and Mark A. Cheetham, 131–50. Ann Arbor: University of Michigan Press, 1990.

Banville, John. *Athena*. London: Secker and Warburg, 1995.

———. *The Book of Evidence*. London: Secker and Warburg, 1984.

———. *Ghosts*. London: Secker and Warburg, 1993.

———. Interview by Eleanor Wachtel. *Writers and Co.* Canadian Broadcasting Company, January 9, 1994.

Birkerts, Sven. *The Gutenberg Elegies: The Fate of Reading in an Electronic Age*. New York: Fawcett Columbine, 1994.

Blake, William. *The Complete Poetry and Prose of William Blake*. Ed. David Erdman. Berkeley: University of California Press, 1982.

Blanchot, Maurice. "Dreaming, Writing." In *Nights as Day, Days as Night*, ed. Michel Leiris, trans. Richard Seiburth, xix–xxviii. Hygiene, Colo.: Eridanos, 1987.

———. "Reading." In *The Gaze of Orpheus and Other Literary Essays*, 91–98. Barrytown, N.Y.: Station Hill, 1981.

————. *The Space of Literature*. Trans. Ann Smock. Lincoln: University of Nebraska Press, 1982.

Blinderman, Barry. "The Compression of Time: An Interview with David Wojnarowicz." In *David Wojnarowicz: Tongues of Flame*, ed. Barry Blinderman, 49–63. New York: Distributed Art Publishers, 1990.

Bloch, Ernst. *Essays on the Philosophy of Music*. Trans. Peter Palmer. Cambridge: Cambridge University Press, 1985.

————. *The Principle of Hope*. Trans. P. Knight, N. Plaice, and S. Plaice. Cambridge: MIT Press, 1986.

Bonnefoy, Yves. "Lifting Our Eyes from the Page." Trans. John Naughton. *Critical Inquiry* 16 (Summer 1990): 796–806.

Brontë, Charlotte. *Shirley*. Harmondsworth, England: Penguin, 1978 [1849].

Brossard, Nicole. *Picture Theory*. Trans. Barbara Godard. Montreal: Guernica, 1991.

Byron, George Gordon. *Don Juan*. Ed. T. G. Steffan, E. Steffan, and W. W. Pratt. London: Penguin, 1987 [1823].

Calvino, Italo. *The Baron in the Trees*. Trans. Archibald Colquhoun. San Diego: Harcourt Brace Jovanovich, 1977.

————. *If on a Winter's Night a Traveller*. Trans. William Weaver. Toronto: Lester and Orpen Dennys, 1986.

Castle, Terry. *The Female Thermometer: Eighteenth-Century Culture and the Invention of the Uncanny*. New York: Oxford University Press, 1995.

————. "Phantasmagoria: Spectral Technology and the Metaphorics of Modern Reverie." *Critical Inquiry* 15 (1988): 26–61.

————. "The Spectralization of the Other in *The Mysteries of Udolpho*." In *The New Eighteenth Century*, ed. Laura Brown and Felicity Nussbaum, 231–53. New York: Methuen, 1987.

Celati, Gianni. "Readers of Books Are Ever More False." In *Appearances*, trans. Stuart Hood, 61–96. London: Serpent's Tail, 1991.

Christensen, Jerome. *Coleridge's Blessed Machine of Language*. Ithaca, N.Y.: Cornell University Press, 1981.

Cixous, Hélène. "Fiction and Its Phantoms: A Reading of Freud's *Das Unheimliche* (The 'Uncanny')." *New Literary History* 7, no. 3 (1976): 525–48.

Clark, David L. "Against Theological Technology: Blake's 'Equivocal Worlds.'" In *New Romanticisms: Theory and Critical Practice*, ed. David L. Clark and Donald C. Goellnicht. Toronto: University of Toronto Press, 1994.

Coleridge, Samuel T. *Biographia Literaria*. Ed. J. Shawcross. London: Oxford University Press, 1958.

————. *The Collected Works of Samuel Taylor Coleridge*. Ed. Kathleen Coburn. Princeton, N.J.: Princeton University Press, 1969.

————. *The Notebooks of Samuel Taylor Coleridge*. Ed. Kathleen Coburn. New York: Pantheon, 1957.

Collier, Peter. "Lire 'Voyelles.'" *Parade sauvage: Revue d'etudes rimbaldiennes* 5 (1989): 56–102.

Collins, Christopher. "Groundless Figures: Reader Response to Verbal Imagery." *The Critic* 51: 11–29.

———. *The Poetics of the Mind's Eye: Literature and the Psychology of the Imagination.* Philadelphia: University of Pennsylvania Press, 1991.

———. *Reading the Written Image: Verbal Play, Interpretation, and the Roots of Iconophobia.* University Park: Pennsylvania State University Press, 1991.

———. "Writing and the Nature of the Supernatural Image, or Why Ghosts Float." In *Languages of Visuality: Crossings Between Science, Art, Politics, and Literature*, ed. Beate Allert, 242–61. Detroit: Wayne State University Press, 1996.

Cortázar, Julio. "Continuity of Parks." In *End of the Game and Other Stories*, trans. Paul Blackburn, 63–65. New York: Random House, 1967.

Darwin, Erasmus. *The Loves of the Plants.* 1789. Reprint, Oxford: Woodstock, 1991.

Defoe, Daniel. *Serious Reflections During the Life and Surprising Adventures of Robinson Crusoe.* London: Constable, 1925.

de Man, Paul. *The Resistance to Theory.* Minneapolis: University of Minneapolis Press, 1986.

Derrida, Jacques. "Living On / BORDER LINES." Trans. James Hulbert. In Harold Bloom et al., *Deconstruction and Criticism*, 75–176. New York: Seabury, 1979.

———. *Memoirs of the Blind: The Self-Portrait and Other Ruins.* Trans. Pascale-Anne Brault and Michael Naas. Chicago: University of Chicago Press, 1993.

———. *Memoires for Paul de Man.* Trans. Eduardo Cadava, Jonathan Culler, and Cecile Lindsay. New York: Columbia University Press, 1986.

———. *Specters of Marx: The State of the Debt, the Work of Mourning, and the New International.* Trans. Peggy Kamuf. New York: Routledge, 1987.

———. "Structure, Sign, and Play in the Discourse of Human Sciences." In *Writing and Difference*, trans. Alan Bass, 278–93. Chicago: University of Chicago Press, 1978.

———. *The Truth in Painting.* Trans. Geoff Bennington and Ian McLeod. Chicago: University of Chicago Press, 1987.

Duroche, Leo. "The Fragmented Self in Michael Ende's *Neverending Story*." Unpublished paper, 1992.

Eco, Umberto. *Six Walks in the Fictional Woods.* Cambridge: Harvard University Press, 1994.

Ende, Michael. *The Neverending Story.* Trans. Ralph Manheim. New York: Penguin, 1984.

Esrock, Ellen. *The Reader's Eye: Visual Imaging as Reader Response.* Baltimore: Johns Hopkins University Press, 1994.

Flaxman, Rhoda. *Victorian Word-Painting and Narrative: Toward the Blending of Genres.* Ann Arbor, Mich.: UMI Research Press, 1987.

Flint, Kate. *The Woman Reader, 1837–1914.* Oxford: Clarendon, 1993.

Foster, Stephen C. "Lettrism: A Point of Views." *Visible Language* 17, no. 3 (1983): 7–12.

Foucault, Michel. "Fantasia of the Library." In *Language, Counter-Memory, Practice: Selected Essays and Interviews,* trans. Donald F. Bouchard and Sherry Simon, ed. Donald F. Bouchard, 87–109. Ithaca, N.Y.: Cornell University Press, 1977.

———. *The Order of Things.* London: Tavistock, 1970.

———. *This Is Not a Pipe.* Trans. James Harkness. Berkeley: University of California Press, 1982.

Freud, Sigmund. *The Interpretation of Dreams.* Vols. 4 and 5 of *The Standard Edition of the Complete Psychological Works of Sigmund Freud.* Trans. James Strachey. London: Hogarth, 1955.

———. *Introductory Lectures on Psycho-analysis* (1915–16). *The Standard Edition of the Complete Psychological Works of Sigmund Freud.* Vols. 15 and 16. Trans. James Strachey. London: Hogarth, 1975.

———. *The Origins of Psychoanalysis.* Trans. Eric Mosbacher and James Strachey. Ed. Marie Bonaparte, Anna Freud, and Ernst Kris. London: Imago, 1954.

———. "The Uncanny." In *The Standard Edition of the Complete Psychological Works of Sigmund Freud,* trans. James Strachey, vol. 17, 218–52. London: Hogarth, 1955.

Gadamer, Hans-Georg. *Truth and Method.* New York: Seabury, 1975.

Galton, Sir Francis. *Inquiries into Human Faculty and its Development.* London: Eugenics Society, 1951 [1883].

Galyon, Linda. "Puttenham's *Enargeia* and *Energeia*: New Twists for Old Terms." *Philological Quarterly* 60, no. 1 (Winter 1981): 31.

Gandelman, Claude. "'The Artist as Traumarbeiter': Sketches of Dreams by Marcel Proust." *Yale French Studies* 84 (1994): 118–35.

Gardner, John. *The Art of Fiction.* New York: Vintage, 1983.

———. *Mickelsson's Ghosts.* New York: Vintage, 1985.

———. *On Moral Fiction.* New York: Basic, 1978.

Gass, William. *Fiction and the Figures of Life.* New York: Knopf, 1970.

———. *On Being Blue.* Boston: Godine, 1976.

Genette, Gérard. *Paratexts: Thresholds of Interpretation.* Trans: Jane E. Lewin. Cambridge: Cambridge University Press, 1997.

Gibson, J. J. *The Senses Considered as Perceptual Systems.* Boston: Houghton Mifflin, 1966.

Greenaway, Peter. *Prospero's Books: A Film of Shakespeare's Tempest.* London: Chatto and Windus, 1991.

Grinstein, Alexander. *On Sigmund Freud's Dreams.* Detroit: Wayne State University Press, 1968.

Grosz, Elizabeth. *Jacques Lacan: A Feminist Introduction.* London: Routledge, 1990.

Halliday, M. A. K. *Explorations in the Fictions of Language*. London: Edward Arnold, 1973.

Handke, Peter. *Absence*. Trans. Ralph Manheim. New York: Farrar, Straus, and Giroux, 1990.

———. *Across*. Trans. Ralph Manheim. New York: Farrar, Straus, and Giroux, 1986.

Hemingway, Ernest. *A Moveable Feast*. New York: Scribner, 1964.

Heppner, Christopher. "Blake as Humpty Dumpty: The Verbal Specification of Visual Meaning." In *Word and Visual Imagination: Studies in the Interaction of English Literature and the Visual Arts*, ed. Karl Josef Holtgen, Peter M. Daly, and Wolfgang Lottes, 223–40. Nuremberg, Germany: Erlangen, 1988.

———. "The Chamber of Prophecy: Blake's 'A Vision' (Butlin #756) Interpreted." *Blake: An Illustrated Quarterly* 25, no. 3 (1991–92): 127–31.

Hunter, I. M. L. *Memory*. Baltimore: Penguin, 1968.

Ingarden, Roman. *The Cognition of the Literary Work of Art*. Trans. Ruth Ann Crowley and Kenneth R. Olsen. Evanston, Ill.: Northwestern University Press, 1973.

Ionesco, Eugène. *Fragments of a Journal*. Trans. Jean Stewart. New York: Grove, 1968.

Irigaray, Luce. *Speculum of the Other Woman*. Trans: Gillian C. Gill. Ithaca, N.Y.: Cornell University Press, 1985.

Iser, Wolfgang. *The Act of Reading: A Theory of Aesthetic Response*. Baltimore: Johns Hopkins University Press, 1974.

———. "The Reading Process: A Phenomenological Approach." In *New Directions in Literary History*, ed. Ralph Cohen, 125–45. Baltimore: Johns Hopkins University Press, 1968.

Jacobi, Carl. "Revelations in Black." In *The Penguin Book of Vampire Stories*, ed. Alan Ryan, 282–300. London: Penguin, 1988.

Jameson, Fredric. "Imaginary and Symbolic in Lacan: Marxism, Psychoanalytic Criticism, and the Problem of the Subject." *Yale French Studies* 55/56 (1977): 338–95.

Jarman, Derek. *Chroma*. London: Century, 1994.

Kames, Henry Home. *The Elements of Criticism*. Hildesheim, Germany: Georg Olms Verlag, 1970.

Kandinsky, Wassily. *Concerning the Spiritual in Art*. Trans. M. T. H. Sadler. New York: Dover, 1977.

Kant, Immanuel. *Kant's Critique of Aesthetic Judgement*. Trans. James Creed Meredith. Oxford: Clarendon Press, 1911.

Kilgour, Maggie. *From Communism to Cannibalism: An Anatomy of Metaphors of Incorporation*. Princeton, N.J.: Princeton University Press, 1990.

Koestler, Arthur. *The Act of Creation*. New York: Macmillan, 1964.

Kosslyn, Stephen. *Ghosts in the Machine: Creating and Using Images in the Brain.* New York: Norton, 1983.

Kuhn, Anna. *Christa Wolf's Utopian Vision: From Marxism to Feminism.* Cambridge: Cambridge University Press, 1988.

Lacan, Jacques. "The Agency of the Letter in the Unconscious, or Reason Since Freud." In *Ecrits: A Selection*, trans. Alan Sheridan, 146–78. New York: Norton, 1977.

———. *The Four Fundamental Concepts of Psycho-Analysis.* Trans. Alan Sheridan. Harmondsworth: Penguin, 1979.

———. "Of Structure as an Inmixing of Otherness Prerequisite to Any Subject Whatsoever." In *The Structuralist Controversy: The Language of Criticism and the Sciences of Man*, ed. Eugenio Donato and Richard Macksey, 186–95. Baltimore: Johns Hopkins University, 1970.

———. *Scilicet* 2–3 (1970).

Lawler, James. *Rimbaud's Theatre of the Self.* Cambridge: Harvard University Press, 1992.

Lippard, Lucy R. "Passenger on the Shadows." *Aperture* 137 (Fall 1994): 6–26.

Marr, David. *Vision: A Computational Investigation into the Human Representation and Processing of Visual Information.* San Francisco: W. H. Freeman, 1982.

Mavromatis, Andreas. *Hypnagogia: The Unique State of Consciousness Between Wakefulness and Sleep.* London: Routledge, 1991.

McKenna, Andrew J. "Lex Icon: Freud and Rimbaud." *Visible Language* 14, no. 3: 219–40.

Merleau-Ponty, Maurice. "Eye and Mind." Trans. Carleton Dallery. In *The Primacy of Perception*, ed. James H. Edie, 159–90. Evanston, Ill.: Northwestern University Press, 1964.

———. *The Visible and the Invisible.* Trans. Alphonso Lingis. Ed. Claude LeFort. Evanston, Ill.: Northwestern University Press, 1968.

Miller, Andrew H. "The Specters of Dickens's Study." *Narrative* 5 (1997): 322–41.

Miller, J. Hillis. "The Critic as Host." In Harold Bloom et al., *Deconstruction and Criticism*, 217–53. New York: Seabury, 1979.

———. "The Figure in the Carpet." *Poetics Today* 1, no. 3 (1980): 107–18.

———. *Illustration.* Cambridge: Harvard University Press, 1992.

Mitchell, W. J. T. *Picture Theory.* Chicago: University of Chicago Press, 1994.

Moberly, L. G. "Inexplicable." In *Strange Tales from the Strand*, comp. Jack Adrian, 183–96. Oxford: Oxford University Press, 1991.

Moritz, William. "The Films of Oskar Fischinger." *Film Culture* 58–60 (1974): 37–188.

Nabokov, Vladimir. *Bend Sinister.* New York: Time-Life, 1964.

———. *Lectures on Literature.* Ed. Fredson Bowers. New York: Harcourt Brace Jovanovich, 1980.

———. *Speak, Memory: An Autobiography Revisited.* New York: McGraw-Hill, 1973.

————. *Strong Opinions*. New York: McGraw-Hill, 1973.

Nell, Victor. *Lost in a Book*. New Haven, Conn.: Yale University Press, 1988.

Olds, Marshall. "Hallucination and Point of View in *La Tentation de Saint Antoine*." *Nineteenth-Century French Studies* 17, nos. 1–2: 170–85.

Ortega y Gasset, José. "Notes on the Novel." In *The Dehumanization of Art, and Other Essays on Art, Culture, and Literature*, trans. Helene Weyl, 57–103. Princeton, N.J.: Princeton University Press, 1968.

Paivio, Allan. "The Mind's Eye in Arts and Science." *Poetics* 12 (1983): 1–18.

Pater, Walter. "Apollo in Picardy." In *Miscellaneous Studies*. New York and London: Macmillan, 1895.

Pearce, Donald. "'Kubla Khan' in Context." *Studies in English Literature* 21, no. 4 (1981): 565–83.

Perkins, David. "Romantic Reading as Revery." *European Romantic Review* 4, no. 2 (1994): 183–94.

Phelan, Peggy. *Unmarked: The Politics of Performance*. London: Routledge, 1993.

Phillips, Tom. *A Humument: A Treated Victorian Novel*. London: Thames and Hudson, 1987.

————. *Works and Texts*. London: Thames and Hudson, 1987.

Potter, Dennis. *Hide and Seek*. London: Faber and Faber, 1990.

Poulet, Georges. "Criticism and the Experience of Interiority." In *The Languages of Criticism and the Sciences of Man: The Structuralist Controversy*, ed. Eugenio Donato and Richard Macksey, 56–72. Baltimore: Johns Hopkins University Press, 1970.

Preston, Kerrison. *The Blake Collection of W. Graham Robertson*. London: Faber and Faber, 1952.

Pullinger, Kate, and Julian Rothenstein, eds. *The Writer's Drawing Book*. London: Redstone, 1994.

Ragland-Sullivan, Ellie. *Jacques Lacan and the Philosophy of Psychoanalysis*. Urbana: University of Illinois Press, 1986.

————. "The Magnetism Between Reader and Text: Prolegomena to a Lacanian Poetics." *Poetics* 12 (1984): 381–406.

Rapaport, Herman. *Between the Sign and the Gaze*. Ithaca, N.Y.: Cornell University Press, 1994.

Reid, Martine, ed. *Boundaries: Writing and Drawing. Yale French Studies* 84 (1994).

Rimbaud, Arthur. *Œuvres*. Ed. S. Bernard and A. Guyaux. Paris: Garnier, 1987.

Rosenblum, Robert. *Transformations in Late Eighteenth-Century Art*. Princeton, N.J.: Princeton University Press, 1969.

Sawka, Jan. *A Book of Fiction*. New York: Clarkson N. Potter, 1986.

Scarry, Elaine. "On Vivacity: The Difference Between Daydreaming and Imagining-Under-Authorial-Instruction." *Representations* 52 (1995): 1–26.

Schaffer, Elinor. "Illusion and Imagination: Derrida's Parergon and Coleridge's Aids to Reflection. Revisionary Readings of Kantian Formalist Aesthetics." In

Aesthetic Illusion: Theoretical and Historical Approaches, ed. Frederick Burwick and Walter Pape, 138–57. New York: William de Gruyter, 1990.

Schneider, Elizabeth. *Coleridge, Opium, and Kubla Khan.* Chicago: University of Chicago Press, 1953.

Seifried, Thomas. "Gazing on Life's Page: Perspectival Vision in Tolstoy." *PMLA* 113, no. 3 (1998): 436–48.

Silverman, Kaja. *The Threshold of the Visible World.* New York: Routledge, 1996.

Skinner, B. F. *Particulars of My Life.* New York: Knopf, 1976.

Sommer, Robert. *The Mind's Eye: Imagery in Everyday Life.* New York: Delacorte, 1978.

Sorrentino, Gilbert. *Mulligan Stew.* New York: Grove, 1979.

Squiers, Carol, ed. *The Critical Image: Essays in Contemporary Photography.* Seattle: Bay, 1990.

Talbot, Michael. *The Holographic Universe.* New York: Harper Collins, 1991.

Thévoz, Michel. "Dubuffet: The Nutcracker." *Yale French Studies* 84 (1994): 29–42.

Tisseron, Serge. "All Writing Is Drawing: The Spatial Development of the Manuscript." *Yale French Studies* 84 (1994): 29–42.

Todorov, Tzvetan. *The Fantastic: A Structural Approach to a Literary Genre.* Trans. Richard Howard. Cleveland: Case Western Reserve University Press, 1973.

Valéry, Paul. "Degas, dance, dessin." In *Œuvres complètes*, 1163–1240. Paris: Gallimard, 1970.

Weber, Samuel. *The Legend of Freud.* Minneapolis: University of Minnesota Press, 1978.

Wilbur, Ken, ed. *The Holographic Paradigm and Other Paradoxes.* Boston: Shambhala, 1985.

Winnard, Andrew. "'These Drowsy Approaches of Sleep': Christa Wolf and the Hypnagogic Dream." *New German Studies* 14, no. 3: 171–86.

Wojnarowicz, David. *Close to the Knives: A Memoir of Disintegration.* New York: Vintage, 1991.

———. *Memories That Smell Like Gasoline.* San Francisco: Artspace, 1992.

Wolf, Christa. *The Author's Dimension: Selected Essays.* Ed. Alexander Stephan. Trans. Jan Van Huerck. New York: Farrar, Straus, and Giroux, 1993.

———. *Cassandra: A Novel and Four Essays.* Trans. Jan Van Huerck. London: Virago, 1984.

———. *What Remains and Other Stories.* Trans. Heike Schwarzbauer and Rick Takvorian. New York: Farrar, Straus, and Giroux, 1993.

Woolf, Virginia. *Collected Essays.* Vol. 1. London: Hogarth, 1966.

———. *The Moment and Other Essays.* London: Hogarth, 1964.

———. *To the Lighthouse.* Harmondsworth, England: Penguin, 1968.

Wordsworth, William. *The Fourteen-Book Prelude.* Ed. W. J. B. Owen. Ithaca, N.Y.: Cornell University Press, 1985.

Index

In this index an "f" after a number indicates a separate reference on the next page, and an "ff" indicates separate references on the next two pages. A continuous discussion over two or more pages is indicated by a span of page numbers, e.g., "57–59." *Passim* is used for a cluster of references in close but not consecutive sequence.

Sontag, Susan, 38
Sorrentino, Gilbert, 67f
specter, 115, 159n36
spectrum, 111, 159n36
Stevens, Wallace, 56
structure, 61, 93, 100, 104, 142, 153n11;
    and language, 27, 35, 46, 51–53, 148
subject and object, 9, 13, 15, 17, 72
subjectivity, 8–14 *passim*
subvision, 121–24, 129ff
supernatural, the, 15ff
symbolic, the, 35f, 47, 134
synesthesia, 156n15

Talbot, Michael, 140, 161n34
Tatham, Frederick, 115
theme, 15f, 57, 68, 158n31
threshold state, *see* liminality
Tisseron, Serge, 81f
Todorov, Tsvetan, 15ff
trait, 81f, 112–15, 119

Uccello, Paolo, 47f
uncanny, the, 17–20, 152n15
unconscious, 26, 71f, 123, 127, 130, 147;
    in reading, 4, 35, 148, 154n27; Freud-
    ian, 6, 24, 34, 36, 40, 46; linguistic, 27,
    31, 36, 51f, 153n11, 156n21; visuality of,
    27, 34, 36, 40, 46; Lacanian, 27, 34ff,
    51f, 70, 153n14. *See also under* words

Valéry, Paul, 81
visibility, 71–80 *passim*, 80, 85, 99, 111ff,
    119ff, 133–36, 152n20, 156n21

vision, 15, 21, 43–46 *passim*, 60, 74ff,
    120–25 *passim*, 129–32 *passim*, 139, 144,
    159n36; vs. visualization, 6, 121; in
    dreams, 36, 103; in "Kubla Khan,"
    103f, 110f. *See also* vision, inner; vision,
    physical
vision, inner, 15, 99, 111f, 119. *See also*
    mental image
vision, physical, 21, 62ff, 76, 99, 111f, 133,
    140, 152n20
visualization, 1–7 *passim*, 30, 60, 64–68
    passim, 73, 77, 80, 121, 138

Wahrnehmungszeichen, 35
wish, 30, 34, 139, 147
Wittgenstein, Ludwig, 141f
Wojnarowicz, David, 121–31, 160n7
Wolf, Christa, 40–46, 139, 154n29
Woolf, Virginia, 3, 39, 69f
word-painting, 77
words, 17, 32, 44, 50–53, 58–60, 70–72,
    113, 136, 141f; as liminal, 4, 25, 40, 50;
    and images, 4ff, 14, 26, 32f, 43–48
    passim, 59ff, 73, 115, 127, 132f, 154n33;
    possession by, 8, 20; and the uncon-
    scious, 26f, 31, 34f, 52; and colors,
    78–80
Wordsworth, William, 32, 104, 130, 133f,
    136
writing, 35, 43, 50, 96; as instruction, 4,
    20; as dreaming, 26, 140; as forest, 50,
    59, 93; as drawing, 81f, 112, 114; and
    reading, 107ff, 113; and the generation
    of images, 108, 156n26

Cultural Memory | *in the Present*

Peter Schwenger, *Fantasm and Fiction: On Textual Envisioning*

Didier Maleuvre, *Museum Memories: History, Technology, Art*

Jacques Derrida, *Monolingualism of the Other; or, The Prosthesis of Origin*

Andrew Baruch Wachtel, *Making a Nation, Breaking a Nation: Literature and Cultural Politics in Yugoslavia*

Niklas Luhmann, *Love as Passion: The Codification of Intimacy*

Mieke Bal, ed., *The Practice of Cultural Analysis: Exposing Interdisciplinary Interpretation*

Jacques Derrida and Gianni Vattimo, eds., *Religion*

Library of Congress Cataloging-in-Publication Data

Schwenger, Peter
    Fantasm and fiction : on textual envisioning / Peter Schwenger.
      p.   cm. — (Cultural memory in the present)
    Includes bibliographical references (p.) and index.
    ISBN 0-8047-3343-0 (alk. paper). — ISBN 0-8047-3472-0
(pbk. : alk. paper)
    1. Fiction.   2. Imagination.   3. Psychoanalysis and literature.
I. Title. II. Series.
PN3331.S444   1999
808.3—dc21   98-50953

 ⊗ This book is printed on acid-free, recycled paper.

Original printing 1999
Last figure below indicates year of this printing:
08   07   06   05   04   03   02   01   00   99